LEAVE NOTHING LEFT

SERVING GOD
AND THE CHINESE
HOUSE CHURCH

THE LIFE AND MINISTRY OF
BARNABAS YOUNG

Leave Nothing Left website: http://www.leavenothingleft.com
Contact us at: info@leavenothingleft.com

DISCLAIMERS

I am liable for the contents of this book, especially the political aspect, which has nothing to do with my friends who have placed their names in this book.

"Barnabas" is the name I use for my ministry work. It is neither my given Chinese name nor my English name. However, it is important to use my work name for security reasons as well, as it is the name by which many people in both the West and East know me.

Some names in the book have been changed for security reasons. Changed names are denoted by an asterisk. Most notably, Barnabas' ministry will be referred to as "the HC Ministry," short for "House Church Ministry." The Christian camp in Hong Kong is also not named for security reasons.

All proceeds from the sale of this book go to support ministry work in China. We do not deduct any administration fees. Part of the cost to print this book has been covered by good friends who support our ministry.

FAMILY ACKNOWLEDGMENTS

Cover design: Barnabas' younger son

Proofreading and editing: Christine*, Barnabas'
daughter-in-law

Translation of endorsements from Chinese to English:
Barnabas' older son

CONTENTS

DEDICATION

This book is affectionately dedicated to
My Lord.
May the readers only see You when they read this book.
May Your name be glorified.

Also, to my family (Young & So),
Who love Jesus, our Lord and Savior,
Who believe there are miracles when God is present,
Who are willing to pay the price to follow Jesus.

Finally,
Special thanks to my granddaughter, who has inspired me
so much although she is only three years old. She never
walks, but is always running when she is on the ground.

願你吸引我、我們就快跑跟隨你! 雅歌 1:4

Draw me, we will run after thee. Song of Songs 1:4 (KJV)

ENDORSEMENTS

Endorsements are listed in no particular order.

Ministry Partners

Barnabas is one of my dearest friends, as well as someone with whom I have served for the past thirty years. Although our upbringings and circumstances are vastly different, Barnabas has chosen to walk alongside us and abide with us. He willingly walks the Way of the Cross along with the Chinese House Church, becoming a member of the mainland church. He loves God, is humble and calm, can endure great hardship, is honest and does not patronize, is loving and passionate, and is truly an honorable example for us all.

Barnabas has seen it all during the past several decades working with the Chinese House Church. He has both experienced and witnessed numerous stages and difficulties of the church: initial planting, revival, persecution, development, and transition. His partnership, presence, offering, sacrifice, and participation brought forth great love in our daily life and ministry.

His words and actions are simple and practical, his life is legendary, his ministry is outstanding, and his testimony in his book is truthful.

The testimony and stories in his book are written with his sweat, tears, and blood. It is my privilege to write this endorsement, and I am most pleased to introduce this book to you and your friends. May the Lord bless you and direct you through this book, as well as introduce many aspects of Barnabas' ministry. May the Lord use this book to cultivate many more saintly lives.

—申先锋 Joshua Shen
House Church Movement Leader in China

On the road of faith, many like to put icing on the cake and engage the harvest, but few are willing to sow seeds and come to the aid of those with desperate needs. The spirits of many ignite for but a moment as their passion dwindles away quickly, while few hearts sustain their steadfast devotion. Many are willing to offer words of encouragement, but few offer helping hands. Thank you, Barnabas, for your ongoing and unceasing support in all areas. May the Lord bless you and your entire family!

—GM
House Church Movement Leader in China

The Bible teaches that a bondservant is a committed disciple of Christ who unreservedly dedicates their life to serving the Master. They fully realize that their decision to serve Christ also calls them to forfeit their personal rights, comfort, safety, and human desires to the will of Jesus. I have had the distinct honor of knowing such an individual from China for over twenty-five years. His name is Barnabas, and he is a man after God's own heart. This book, which describes his life and call to ministry, is a must-read for every believer who seeks to understand what goes into the making of a Christian bondservant.

—RON PEARCE
President/Founder,
Empower Ministries International

Leave Nothing Left is a must-read book! Knowing Barnabas and having traveled with him throughout various places in China for the past twenty years allows me to personally attest to his passion for sharing the gospel, bringing glory to God, and demonstrating humble Christ-like service like few people I've ever known. I believe God has used Barnabas as a true catalyst for the spread of Christianity in 21st-century China! His unique conversion story and subsequent influence and networking capability with gospel movement leaders gives him an unprecedented platform to tell the story of God's work in China as few others can. While reading Barnabas' stories, you will be brought to tears and, at other times, laugh out loud at the unbelievable circumstances God put on his heart to share with his readers. Get ready for God to give you a bigger vision for His work in China and a more dedicated heart to serve Him wherever you are.

—DR. LARRY A. VOLD
Pastor

If you like the book of Acts, you are going to love this book! This book portrays the acts of the Holy Spirit lived out through God's humble servant and my good friend, Barnabas, whom I've known for over twenty years. Discover how God raises up one person to impact the least of these as well as the entire nation of China for Christ. Barnabas introduced me to the suffering but victorious Chinese House Church movement on a trip to mainland China that absolutely changed my life and the course of my ministry. During that trip and several others, I have fallen in love with so many Chinese brothers and sisters whom I consider modern-day heroes of the faith. Prepare for a life-changing and possibly ministry-altering experience. You will be encouraged, blessed, challenged, and inspired to be God's servant to your world. Thank you, Barnabas for your example and friendship.

—DR. MARK TEYLER
President, 360Serve

What kind of man does it take to minister to a group of believers who continually endure hardship and rejection? What kind of man understands the depths of their pain and isolation? Does he understand the sense of God's calling that drives these believers to serve the Lord in the face of intense hostility? Does he have that sense of God's calling as well? The story of Barnabas' life is a story of God's grace in the midst of hardship. It is a story of love for the marginalized of China, the House Church. From the preparation of his childhood in the experiences of hardship to his humble service among Chinese believers, Barnabas' life is a testimony of a great God who loves and cares for his children in China.

—Dr. George Cannon
Pastor

This book is a testimony to the greatness and goodness of our God, and an assurance that our God is sovereign and faithful.

I am so thankful to God for the author, a humble servant of the Lord and my dear friend in Christ. To read about the transformation that God has brought about in his life, and the works that God has done and is still accomplishing through his life—especially in one of the more challenging places like China—does sincerely invite my heart to praise and celebrate our God, and tremendously encourages me to trust and obey God more and more. As God has used this book to bless me, I am sure that He will use this book to bless you, the readers, too.

For Yours is the kingdom and the power and the glory forever. Amen.

—Prasit Mungkaka
Lawyer in Bangkok, Thailand

I have known the author for more than forty years. We worked and were roommates together at a Christian camp when we were young. We became fast friends, and we both have joined the pastoral ranks since then. Although we don't get to see each other very often due to our busy lives, our friendship and trust remains. When we do have opportunities to get together, we talk openly about everything like old friends.

Reading Barnabas' book brought back many memories for me as well. When I first got to know him as a teenager, he was very quiet and spoke few words. He kept many things to himself at the time but always worked hard, seriously, sincerely, and trustworthily and held fast to godly principles. I am certain that upon reading this book, you will feel the same about Barnabas.

In his book, Barnabas shared about his difficult childhood growing up in a seaside fishing village but was greatly moved by the great love of Christ and subsequently committed his life to the Lord. He was called to China and dedicated his life to serve the Chinese House Church and has encountered many difficulties and trials. But he was simply being refined by God to better serve Him and His people. Through his faith and determination, Barnabas humbly relied on God as he served those around him.

Having finished his book, I am in awe of our God who so loves his people. As the Bible said in Nehemiah 13:2, "Our God, however, turned the curse into a blessing," as well as in Psalms 8:4, "what is man that you are mindful of him, or the son of man that you care for him?" May the Lord greatly use the words written by the author to encourage and bless the readers.

—REV. TIM SAU YIU
Pastor, Former General Secretary,
A Church Denomination in Hong Kong

The story of Barnabas' life that is shared in this book is a great and glorious recounting of how God chooses a seemingly insignificant and obscure orphan born on a fishing boat in the South China Sea, saves him, gives him a new heart and desires, and then uses him to build and minister to Christ's Church in

China. Hearing how God graciously and sovereignly continues to grow His Church by putting people, resources, and circumstances together to expand His kingdom in the face of severe spiritual opposition and difficult physical circumstances is amazing. This story is truly inspiring and reminds us that God's kingdom will never be thwarted and that He can use the improbable person who humbly submits to and is willing to serve our great Lord and gracious Savior to accomplish what would seem to be impossible from the world's viewpoint. Barnabas humbly tells how our gracious Lord is worthy of all the glory, praise, and adoration for the great things He has done and is currently doing today. Reading this book will lift your spirit and give you a greater love, joy, and faith in our awesome God.

—JOHN & SUSAN BELLIG
Business People

What a great privilege to have met the author and to have shared some of his experiences together. In this book you will meet a man whose passion for building the kingdom in the most adverse circumstances will inspire you to be more for Him. A must-read!

—ROBERT DYCK
Goodon Industries

I have worked with Barnabas for two decades. He is my best friend. Working with him has changed my life and millions of others. His training school in Asia is equipping a new generation of Chinese leaders to take the gospel around the world.

The book that you are about to read tells the story of a modern-day Barnabas whom God is using to spark the greatest explosion of Christianity since the book of Acts. Like his namesake, "Barnabas" isn't his birth name. It is his nickname meaning "son of encouragement" (Acts 4:36). It was the name given to him by the House Church movement leaders three decades ago because "he is a good man full of the Holy Spirit and faith."

Barnabas has supported the church in China over three decades, through persecution, danger, and sleepless nights. He has provided the church with millions of Bibles, training schools, family support while pastors serve time in prison, and has supported them in every other way one can imagine. God is also using Barnabas to bring renewal to the church around the world by reminding us that the book of Acts is still continuing, and revival can happen in our cities and churches too.

Read this book and you will know the story of what God is doing in China. Tell the story by sending a copy to your friend. Become part of the story and join with the HC Ministry* to support their work in China.

—TOM HENRY
Pastor

From the first time we met, I've been amazed by Barnabas' passion for the House Church in China. Since then, I've worked alongside Barnabas in China many times and have seen his dedication and willingness to serve the House Church firsthand, even at risk to his own freedom. His entire life, and this book, are a testimony to how God can take someone with a willing heart— regardless of their background—and use them to make an eternal impact in countless lives. I encourage everyone to read *Leave Nothing Left* and pray for the House Church in China.

—VERNON BREWER
Founder & President, World Help

---

* Name changed for security reasons. In this book, we will refer to Barnabas' ministry as the HC Ministry (short for House Church Ministry).

I'll never forget the day we entered a house church in China. Barnabas held the door open on that cold and rainy day as we entered the home. Awaiting us were forty Christ-followers, huddled in a room with no heat, chairs, or the "things" we think we need for worship…and they were praising God! My heart broke as I realized they only had one Bible to share among them, yet their love and joy for God was overwhelming. What I witnessed that day was simply because one man was willing to "risk it all" to make an eternal difference. *Leave Nothing Left* is his story—one of heartache, faith, compassion and hard work—all for the gospel and the House Church in China. As you read with an open heart, allow God to speak to you, and then pray for the House Church in China.

—TOM THOMPSON
Senior Vice President, World Help

I've had the privilege to call Barnabas my friend for over a decade now. I look up to him as a mentor and am beyond thrilled that he has penned his life story to paper. Through sharing his experiences and insights on the church in China, Barnabas marvelously helps to introduce the reader to how God is working in China and makes it abundantly clear we should all live our lives for God's glory and not our own. This gripping book is a must-read for anyone wanting to better understand the church in China or anyone looking to better understand a true servant-minded model of leadership.

—JEFF WOOD
Director of International Ministries, Turning Point for God

Fond memories of twenty-plus years of shared life, fellowship, ministries, and travel come rushing back as we read *Leave Nothing Left* by our dear brother, Barnabas. Much of what he recalls is familiar to us, while other portions fill in some gaps bringing the picture to wholeness. At the time, little did we know in the day-to-day routines of life what God was doing. That is the life of faith, is it not? Only as we look back do we see more clearly, understand, and articulate the lessons and insights as Barnabas has done here. We serve an awesome God!

This volume reveals the 21st-century workings of Jesus in a life surrendered to Him. He called disciples from among the fishermen on the shores of Galilee in about AD 33, and He had His hand on the orphaned son of a fisherman on the South China Sea in AD 1956 to present day. There are valuable spiritual lessons here, insightful first-hand information about China and Chinese life, heart-stopping adventures, amusing situations, love, and above all revelations of how God works with and among us today.

Thank you, Barnabas, for taking the time to share your life and walk with the Living God in this writing. Thank you for the shared journey. May Jesus Christ be praised!

—PROFESSOR JOSEPH AND MAREE KLINGENSMITH
Servants in Cross-Cultural Ministry

HC MINISTRY BOARD MEMBERS

I first met Barnabas when he was a teenager. He had lived a very hard life up to that point, and he was looking for a place to serve God. He arrived at a Christian youth camp in Hong Kong, and Donna and I became his family very quickly. I knew that he would be a great future director of the Camp. He advanced later to become assistant director and then director. Throughout these years, the camp stayed full of campers, and many of them accepted Christ. He always had a place in his heart for the church in China, and while director of the camp, he started to travel in China and minister to the house churches. I felt that he should be ordained as a pastor for his role in the house churches of China, and that goal was accomplished.

Barnabas has established and planted numerous churches across China. The pastors still call him asking for advice, and Barnabas visits them regularly at great cost to his safety. In addition, we collaborated with a local church leader to set up a training facility for Chinese pastors in Asia, and this has enabled him to serve God both in China and at the facility outside China. Over 7,000 pastors from both house churches and Three-Self churches have been trained in this facility in the last few years. Pastors receive training by very well-known pastors from around the world. Barnabas and his team manage this facility, and his family also works with him. Seldom do you meet an entire family that has immersed themselves in such an endeavor. His family works with the house churches in China as encouragers, and he is an incredible leader. I have traveled with him in China and met leaders from across the country, and they all treat him with great respect and honor. This book will bless you as you learn about the House Church ministry of Barnabas.

—Dr. John Bechtel
Second-Generation Missionary to the Chinese People

_____

Barnabas is a trustworthy servant of the Lord Jesus Christ.

I had the great joy of traversing through various parts of Hong Kong and China with Barnabas. This journey was a survey of the glorious Church that Jesus Christ has established in mainland China. As a young husband and father of three, I had put my life into Barnabas' hands, trusting completely in his protection and care during our journeys.

One aspect of this trip was to consider serving in the work that Barnabas was doing. Immediately it became clear to me that Barnabas had great interest in loving people. He was concerned solely with being the hands and feet of Jesus Christ to me and to the people with whom we interacted.

As we became closer and as I entered into service as treasurer for his operation it was clear that asking for money was certainly not something Barnabas did. This was very refreshing as it enabled the Lord to provide in better ways and it enabled Barnabas to focus on his work.

One time, Barnabas and I traveled to the home of a person who loved the Lord and who was capable of making a large financial impact on the church in China. Barnabas and I prayed together after we arrived. I remember Barnabas saying to the Lord something like this, "Lord, I do not know how to ask for money, so if this man is supposed to give money you tell him to." We never asked for any money and we did not receive much money from this man, but the Lord brought plenty of money in from other places.

While Barnabas does not ask for money, he certainly gives it away. While we were at one underground seminary, I was nearby as the head of the seminary and Barnabas conversed in Chinese (which I do not speak). The man stopped and made sure that Barnabas told me that the funding of the seminary had come from Barnabas. He wanted me to know how generous Barnabas had been and how they could not be where they were without him. Of all the things he could have said to me, it was this one thing.

My sense is that all across the great nation of China there are people who know Barnabas' generosity and his giving heart. I know personally that he is a man of integrity and a man who cares deeply about his family, the great nation of China and sharing the glory of God with everyone with whom he interacts.

I consider my time with Barnabas to have been a blessing from the Lord. Jesus Christ is seated, as King of heaven and earth at the right hand of the Father. He has granted us His Holy Spirit. His enemies are, even now, being fashioned into a footstool for His feet. He has appointed us to do this work. A great fashioner of the enemies into a footstool is Barnabas. Our weapon is not a sword, but love. Barnabas wields this weapon of love faithfully and gracefully. It is an honor to know Barnabas, to serve Barnabas and to call him a friend.

—BRADLEY HILL
Managing Director, The Hill Group, Morgan Stanley

Barnabas' passion for the expansion of God's kingdom in China is exciting and contagious. The Lord has given Barnabas a distinct calling to serve the House Church in China. Barnabas' servant-leadership approach, and willingness to take risks to proclaim the gospel, has led to countless Chinese people professing Christ as Lord. Barnabas serves Chinese churches as a teacher, mentor, advisor and trusted friend. I had the privilege of first meeting Barnabas in December 2008, while I was an American expatriate working in Hong Kong. During our first meeting, I could tell God's hand was on this man and that he was a humble and faithful servant of the Lord. Three weeks after we met, I was fighting for my life after suffering a major stroke. Upon learning of my stroke, Barnabas initiated prayer groups of Chinese Christians from multiple house church movements. A few short days later, God performed a miracle and began healing my brain. Miracles—and God moving in powerful ways—are nothing new to Barnabas and the Chinese House Church. For decades, the Chinese Communist Party has gone to great lengths to control and minimize the House Church in China; however, God has continued to draw millions of new believers to Himself. By adopting a mentality and theology known in China as the Way of the Cross, God has blessed Barnabas and Chinese believers, and allowed them to experience Himself in profound ways. Western believers will be encouraged and amazed at how God has used this humble man in mighty ways.

—CHASE ANDERSON
Businessman

Barnabas is a tireless evangelist and truly lives up to his name, which means "Son of Encouragement." When you spend time with Barnabas, you sense in a very real way someone who has spent a great deal of time with God.

His HC Ministry teaches and trains the pastors that take the gospel message from the heart of the biggest cities to the most remote villages in China. This ministry runs a very lean organization, and I know my gift is being fully utilized and multiplied.

A small Christian camp in Hong Kong has seen thousands of kids come to know Jesus. Read Barnabas' unlikely story of meeting Jesus, how he eventually became the camp director, and how he now leads a ministry that helps to take the gospel message to every village in China and engages churches worldwide.

Barnabas' wife Margaret is a rock. She quietly keeps the family and the home running smoothly while Barnabas is traveling everywhere. Her handicraft business has helped the ministry grow in a very unique way. The HC Ministry has gotten into and stayed in places they would not be able to any other way.

—**MICHAEL GREENFIELD**
Farmer, Business Owner

ACKNOWLEDGEMENTS

I want to acknowledge my best friend, Jesus Christ.

One of my granddaughters always asks me, "Grandpa, will you play with me?" I am very happy to tell her yes, because she wants to spend time with an old man like me. I will drop all my work, or finish my conversation on the phone, and will happily spend time playing with her because I love her so much. I am happy for another opportunity to show her how much I love her.

Jesus, thank You for spending time "playing" with me. When I say "playing," I mean: thank You for spending so much of Your precious time with me and listening to me, even listening to my complaints. Sometimes I say angry words about people around me, and am even angry with You because I think You do not react quick enough to solve my problems. But You always forgive me, and You make me understand more and more what grace and unconditional love are.

You always welcome me and give me a big hug and prepare a big feast for me and my friends, just because I repent and come back to You like the prodigal son (Luke 15:11–32).

Thank You so much for not feeling bored or troubled as I WhatsApp You or call You all day long, asking You so many questions, opinions, directions, and what to do next. For sixty-four years, You have been very patient with me. You never give up on me.

I feel as though I have done nothing right, but still, You correct me in patience and love. You change my heart and make me calm and stable. You know my feelings and always heal my broken heart. Your hands touch me, comfort me, and make me feel secure.

I am not worthy to write this book, but I follow Your lead. I wrote down many real stories of my life through the lens of Your eyes. Without You, I am nothing; with You, I have everything.

You know me inside out, so You know this book is not about me. This book is about how You have molded me so I can be used by You in the work You allow me to do.

Like Your man Job in the Bible, I feel there are times that You are silent. But I have learned that when a teacher gives an exam to his or her students, the teacher must remain silent so the students will go through the test on their own. I am glad I went through many tests in my life with the help of the Holy Spirit. You only keep silent when I am taking the exams. The rest of the time, You teach me in love.

I keep learning how to love You and glorify You. The Way of the Cross is my glory when I serve You. May this book bring glory to You. My Lord Jesus, I love You!

INTRODUCTION

After I became a Christian at the age of fifteen, I started to learn about communism and China. Since 1973, I have read many books about communism, including difficult books like *The Communist Manifesto* (Chinese version), books about Lenin and Stalin, and almost all of Chairman Mao's books. These are not leisure books. They were not fun to read and were difficult to understand when I was younger. But I was eager and interested to learn, because my calling was to work with the House Church in China, a country ruled by atheist communists.

Beginning in 1976, I subscribed to several political magazines in Hong Kong. I still keep some copies of these magazines at home. I read a lot of articles and true stories about life in China. One mainland Chinese author I respect very much from the late 1970s and 1980s is Liu Binyan 劉賓雁. Liu was a famous Chinese author, journalist (*China Daily*), and political dissident. He passed away in the U.S. in 2005 at eighty years old. *People or Monsters* (1979) was the first in a series of works describing and exposing bureaucracy, corruption, and social problems of China under Mao's regime, and was noteworthy for its use of fact-based reporting instead of the pure fiction of the CCP. He wrote, "The Communist Party controls everything except the Communist Party." This sentence caused him many problems, and he was later kicked out of the Chinese Communist Party. *People or Monsters* 《人妖之間》, *A Second Kind of Loyalty* 《第二種忠誠》 (1985), and other essays made him a household name among Chinese readers and cemented his reputation as "China's conscience."

Many of the events in Liu's life are recounted in his memoir, *A Higher Kind of Loyalty* (1985). The first loyalty he described is diligent, hardworking, honest obedience with no objections. This is the common loyalty value we all know.

Liu described the second loyalty as a higher kind of loyalty. He wrote, "Do what you should do, say what you should say."[ii] It is rather simple, but Liu paid an expensive price for writing it, losing his freedom.

I have never forgotten what Liu wrote about a higher kind of loyalty. "Do what I should do and say what I should say" was my guideline and direction when I wrote this book. Yes, I dare to write the book and say only the truth, but I must always ask myself, "What is the truth?" Sometimes we try to find the truth and think we know it, but in reality, we don't. So I know I must always be diligent to find the truth.

What I write in this book is based on truth. Let it speak for itself. Choose to believe me or not. In this book, I am telling you what has happened in my life. I have a great memory. That does not mean I won't be wrong in some cases, but in this book, I am writing about the key issues and events in my life. Some of the details may be blurred, but the facts and feelings are true to me.

In the last twenty-some years, I have worked full time in China. I have worked with churches — especially the house churches — whether urban or rural. I have traveled extensively to every province and special region in China, except Tibet.

House churches in China are regarded as illegal entities. So I have concerns about how much I should write about house churches. I have concerns for my partners in China and overseas. I have concerns for my coworkers and staff and especially my dear family. I ask myself, "What if . . . ?"

In his 1933 inaugural address, Franklin D. Roosevelt said, "The only thing we have to fear is fear itself." Fear is always the most frustrating thing, but the Bible says there is no fear in love. I am not going to live in fear. I have not lived in fear for the last thirty years, and I will continue to trust my Lord to remove my fear.

I think I have the quality of the first loyalty: diligent, hardworking, honest obedience with no objections. As for a higher kind of loyalty, I will have to say what I should say—the true facts without fear. I am going to tell you what I have experienced in China over the last twenty-some years. I trust my Lord will carry me through the valley of the shadow of death. "Even though I walk through the darkest valley, I will fear no evil, for you are with me; your rod and your staff, they comfort me. You prepare a table before me in the presence of my enemies" (Ps. 23).

I also remember reading books of Václav Havel, who was a Czech statesman, writer, and former dissident. He served as the last President of Czechoslovakia from 1989 until the dissolution of Czechoslovakia in 1992 through the famous Velvet Revolution. He served as the first president of the Czech Republic from 1993 to 2003. He was known for his essays, most particularly *The Power of the Powerless*, published in 1978, in which he described a societal paradigm in which citizens were forced to "live within a lie" under the communist regime. The power from the powerless comes from "telling the truth." [iii] As a Christian and a pastor, I obey what my Lord tells me to do, *to tell the truth with love*.

When I was in graduate school, I had to read many Harvard business cases for group discussions, proposals, and papers. When I wasn't reading business cases, I came across a Harvard study of adult development called the Grant Study, which began in 1938 and continued until 2014. When I read the study in 1999, it was still in progress. Dr. Arlie Bock started the study in 1938, and Dr. George Vaillant took over the study in 1967 until it ended in 2014. The study's topic was "Is there an equation for success and victory in life?" [iv]

From 1939 to 1944, 268 male undergraduate students were selected from Harvard University and volunteered for the study. These students were from upper-class, wealthy families. They were smart, ambitious, and well connected. The aim of the study was to prove that students with a wealthy background were more likely to be successful in life.

The students were monitored under ten criteria until they were eighty years old. They were monitored by answering questionnaires, visiting physicians and researchers, as well as interacting with the study managers. Of these men, four became congressmen, one became a state governor, and one became the president of the United States, John Kennedy, (but of course, he was assassinated before he reached eighty years old).

Of the ten criteria used to determine the equation for success and victory in life, two were related to wealth, four were related to physical health, mental health, and family relationships, and four were related to social well-being, social contribution, and acceptance by society.

The seventy-six-year Grant Study's conclusion, the recipe for success, was summarized in a few simple words, "The key to happiness and success in life is love. Full stop." [v] If success is counted only by education, wealth, or ranking in society or political power, then 99.8 percent of the world's population are like me. They will never reach the finish line of success. This research was compiled over seventy-six years, followed the lives of 267 people, and devoted so much effort to discover that the formula for victory in life was not wealth, IQ, or "the good life," but it was actually one word: love!

This answer seems too ordinary to be incredible. Remember, this is not a religious study concluding that this world needs love. There are different kinds of love, but I firmly know that my Lord Jesus Christ conquered the world with love, not with a powerful military.

If you want your children to have a victorious life, give them full love! If you want to have a good career, good friends, and good family, give more love to win the love of others!

I was already looking for love at the age of five. I grew up in a church that was supposed to be a community of love, but it took me ten years until I personally met Jesus face-to-face through the power of the Holy Spirit. Since then, I have been loved by Jesus, and I am trying to love others with the love of Jesus Christ!

The year 2020 is special for me. My birthday will be considered a national secret.* I was sixty-three last year, and next year I will be sixty-five, and I was born in June, so you know my age for this year. I have hesitated about what to write in my book. In China, telling the truth may cost your job or even your life. I know there is no medicine that can cure "regret." There may be sensitive issues, but I am not going to avoid them because of fear of persecution. I know I will not regret telling the truth. I will only regret not telling the truth. I am learning from the house church pastors in China, the Way of the Cross is my glory. I prayed, and I know I need to tell the truth and how my Lord has blessed me all these years. "Be faithful, even to the point of death, and I will give you life as your victor's crown" (Rev. 2:10). I have peace that only the Holy Spirit can give me. When Jesus went back to heaven two thousand years ago, He said, "Peace I leave with you . . . Do not let your hearts be troubled and do not be afraid" (John 14:27).

---

* There was a famous protest in a famous square in China on the day of my birthday. The Chinese government does not allow any discussion about those events and does not recognize that anything happened on that day.

WHAT HAPPENED IN 1956, THE YEAR I WAS BORN

What was happening in the world:

- Despite Britain's claim to have killed 10,000 Mau Mau warriors over the preceding four years, it was losing its battle to retain Kenya as a possession.

- France was also losing its fight to keep colonies in North Africa.

- Hungary tried to revolt against communism, but it was brutally suppressed by Russian tanks.

- Fidel Castro emerged as a dictator in Cuba.

What was happening in China:

- The country had an estimated population of 620 million people.

- The Hundred Flowers Campaign was a program by the Chinese Communist Party (CCP) that encouraged citizens to openly express their opinions of the communist regime. After this brief period of liberalization, Mao cracked down on those who criticized the communist regime. The crackdown continued from 1957–1959.

What was happening in the U.S.A.:

- Top stars in Hollywood were Elvis Presley and Bridget Bardot.

- Eisenhower easily defeated Adlai Stevenson for a second term.

- The U.S. Navy launched the USS Saratoga as the first nuclear carrier.

What was happening in sports:

- Michigan State beat UCLA 17–14 to become the Rose Bowl Champions.

- The NY Yankees beat the Brooklyn Dodgers to win the MLB World Series 4 games to 3.

- In the NFL Championship Game, the NY Giants routed the Chicago Bears 47–7.

- The NFL Player of the Year was Frank Gifford of the NY Giants.

- The NBA champion was the Philadelphia Warriors.

- The Olympic Games were held in Melbourne, Australia.

What was happening at the movies:

- *Around the World in 80 Days* won the Academy Award for Best Picture.

What was happening in the South China Sea and Hong Kong:

- The 1956 Hong Kong protests were the result of escalating provocations between pro-Nationalist and pro-Communist factions in Hong Kong during Double Ten Day, October 10th, 1956.

- A baby boy, Barnabas, was born in a Hong Kong fishing boat in the South China Sea.

Who was also born in 1956:

- Tsai Ing-Wen (President of Taiwan), Tom Hanks, Mel Gibson, Larry Bird, and Joe Montana.

TIMELINE

1899: The Boxer Rebellion

1912: The Republic of China is officially formed.

1921: The Chinese Communist Party is officially formed.

1931: Civil War begins between the Chinese Nationalists and the Chinese Communist Party (CCP).

1937–1945: The Second Sino-Japanese War begins.

1945: The Republic of China is formed in Taiwan.

1949: Communists declare mainland China the People's Republic of China. CCP chairman Mao Zedong becomes China's new leader.

1956: Barnabas is born in Hong Kong.

1958–1962: The Great Leap Forward transforms agricultural China into an industrial system, resulting in 56 million deaths, including 3 million by suicide.

1966: The Cultural Revolution begins. It erases all traces of capitalism, traditional Chinese culture, and religion, replacing it with Maoism.

1972: Richard Nixon becomes the first American president to visit China. Barnabas begins work at a Christian camp in Hong Kong.

September 9, 1976: Mao dies. Deng Xiaoping assumes power for the next two decades.

April 1989: Tiananmen Square protests begin. At least 300 die in the protests.

1989–1995: Barnabas plants three house churches in the southern part of China.

July 1, 1997: Britain returns Hong Kong to China.

April 2000: Barnabas takes his first trip into China specifically for the House Church.

2000: Barnabas begins his forty-nine-hour run through China back to Hong Kong.

November 2001: China joins the World Trade Organization.

May 2008: An 8.0 earthquake hits Sichuan Province, killing at least 69,000. Barnabas & Partners staff travel to Sichuan and provide relief.

2010: HC Ministry is established in Hong Kong.

2011: HC Ministry is established in the United States.

March 2013: Xi Jinping becomes President of China.

2014: The Umbrella Movement begins in Hong Kong, protesting against China's selection of candidates for Hong Kong elections.

February 2018: Passage of Revised Version of the Religious Affairs Regulations

June 2020: Passage of Hong Kong National Security Law

GET TO KNOW THE AUTHOR
For Your Eyes Only

Registered trademark that my ancestors gave me: Young

Name always used: Barnabas

Hormones: M

Nationality: First and most important passport—Heavenly Born-Again passport

Passport for travel: It shows I am American

ID Card: I am a Hong Konger—ethnic Han Chinese

Where I breathed my first breath: The only city in the world that had a deadline in 1997 and has another one in 2047—Hong Kong

Where did I grow up: The same city, which is now part of China. This country is not mine, but I am from this country, where the leaders "never" make a mistake.

Hong Konger's situation in 2020: Hong Kong people are mixed race orphans without parents.

Marital status: One wife, two sons, two daughters-in-law, two granddaughters, one grandson

What is the current status of this machine: This machine has been active for sixty-four years, has been upgrading through walking 15,000 steps a day and inputting healthy food. There is still no need for major renovation, but it will not be able to be set to the default mode anymore.

Education: Ph.D.—Doctor of Science on "worries," taken away in 1972 when the Holy Spirit occupied my heart and mind.

My best friend: Jesus Christ, I know He is not coming to make bad people good; Jesus comes to make dead people live (eternal life).

Favorite foods: All kinds of seafood, steak, homemade Cantonese white-cut chicken (haha, only Cantonese and Hong Kongers will understand what this dish is).

Why do I want to stay alive until my last breath? Life is a struggle, but it is to prove my existence. As long as I am still alive, there are many things to look forward to.

Family motto: Eat when we can. Go to the toilet when there is one. You do not know what will be coming next (from my childhood and our experience in China).

Life mottos:

> *"The world cares very little about what a man or woman knows, it is what the man or woman is able to do that counts!"* (Booker T. Washington)

> *"I do not have any rights to be angry at my God." "The greatest pain is not in suffering, but unwillingness to obey."* (my mottos)

Ministry motto: It is nice to be important, but it is more important to be nice.

My wish: That our Lord, according to His timing, will take down any leaders of the world that do not care for their own people, and will take me down too if I do not serve His people well.

Spiritual encounter: Jesus left the ninety-nine good sheep to seek me. When I get lost in the wilderness, He comes to rescue and deliver me. He loves me passionately and personally.

My favorite Scripture verses:

"Why not put up with wrong? Why not undergo loss?" 1 Corinthians 6:7 (BBE)

「為甚麼不情願受欺呢? 為甚麼不情願喫虧呢?」
哥林多前書6:7

"The spirit of the Lord is on me, because I am marked out by him to give good news to the poor; he has sent me to make the broken-hearted well, to say that the prisoners will be made free, and that those in chains will see the light again." Isaiah 61:1 (BBE)

「主耶和華的靈在我身上; 因為耶和華用膏膏我, 叫我傳好信息給謙卑的人, 差遣我醫好傷心的人, 報告被擄的得釋放, 被囚的出監牢。」 以賽亞書61:1

My wish for the rest of my life: To not create problems for people around me. Simply speaking, I wish not to be a troublemaker.

How I view the current global situation: It is always darkest before dawn. As long as we can survive, there is hope for change. As long as we are still alive, there are many good things to look forward to.

My prayer request: To always manage my time wisely. Also, if I disappear in China, don't do anything except pray for me.

PROLOGUE

It was a hot and sunny day. I was walking down the street, holding my two-year-old granddaughter in my arms. I realized she suddenly felt fearful, so I looked up to see what she saw — a group of six men walking toward us. They meant us no harm, but to her they looked scary. I began to reassure her by lifting her up, her face close to mine, but then to my surprise there was no fear in her face. She simply looked back at me with confidence, knowing I would protect her.

When I was her age, I had no one to protect me. I was an orphan, and I felt like an orphan, alone and looking for love and protection. I vividly remember, as young as five years old, I was desperately searching for love.

Unlike an orphan out of Oliver Twist or some tearful Hollywood movie, I wasn't sad about my fate. But I did have an identity problem. I didn't know who I was. I didn't know who my parents were or from where I came. I was alone with no one to understand me, my secret sorrows, or my difficulties. I didn't know what love really was, or what kind of love I was searching for. But I did know, even from a very young age, that I wanted someone to hug and hold me, just how the moms and dads of other kids would hold them.

I searched for that love and identity until I was fifteen years old. That is when God poured out His unconditional love and acceptance on me at a Christian summer camp (where I didn't even really want to be in the first place!). But when I accepted Christ, I finally knew who I was — I was a child of God. I had a heavenly Father, who gave me not only an identity and purpose in this life, but one for eternity as well.

Now I know my identity. I am a servant of God! As a servant, I do not have any power of my own, nor do I need to fight for control. I do not have any power struggles because I only trust and obey my Lord. My identity is found in Him as I serve Him. Whatever I do, I give all the glory to God.

This is my story, and as I've shared it over the years, I've received many different reactions. Some have told me it's a tragedy. When I hear that, it makes me think of a famous Jewish saying that there is no difference between tragedy and comedy. If you come out of tragedy, it's a comedy. If you're absorbed in a comedy, it's a tragedy. Others tell me my story is special. To be honest, I don't think it's very special in light of the amazing stories of those I serve in China.

What I do know is that my life is not a tragedy. As I count God's blessings in my life and continue to let God master me, my life is a comedy in the best sense. For God has brought me out of tragedy, and I've never looked back. While I don't know how special my story is, many of my friends have asked me to write it down and share it so that others might be encouraged and God might be glorified. Therefore, in the following pages, I'm sharing with you what the Lord has asked of me and has allowed me to do in China for only one reason—to give Him glory. God has blessed me so that I might bless others in return. I want everyone to see God and His wonderful works in my life and throughout all of China.

I've had many failures, and I've learned many important principles through them. I'm always reminded that while winning makes me happy, losing makes me wise. In order to win with the power of my Lord, I humbly serve my Lord with all my heart and give everything to Him—my five loaves and two fishes. One of the greatest presidents of the United States, Abraham Lincoln, said, "Nearly all men can stand adversity, but if you want to test a man's character, give him power." I had no power when I grew up. But as I was worked like a slave, adversity molded my character. After I became a Christian, I learned that Jesus conquered the world with His love, not by military force. He is so powerful with His love and asks us to trust Him. He will fight for us, so we do not need to fight for ourselves. That is why I am still learning to trust my heavenly Father the way my granddaughter trusts me.

As we know, the lives of Christians are not easy. There have been many challenges in my life and there will continue to be many more. I have always thought that my life is like building a house. However, the house is always under construction, and I will never live in a finished house until I get to heaven. In this world, the sky is not always sunny, and the rain falls on us all. It doesn't matter if the weather is beautiful or stormy. What matters is my heart before the Lord. I must do His will as I learn more every day to walk in His will, even though I don't know His plan at the moment.

When you read this book, I hope you see the power of my God, who can change a stubborn and sinful man like me. He can use me, a fisherman's son born in a fishing boat in the South China Sea, to do what He allows me to do. I am glad that at least four of the disciples of Jesus Christ were fishermen. Sometimes, Jesus does not call the qualified. He qualifies those whom He calls.

May this book bring blessings to you. May it encourage you to praise God and grow closer to Him. May it help you find your identity in Him and feel His perfect, eternal, fatherly love.

MAPS

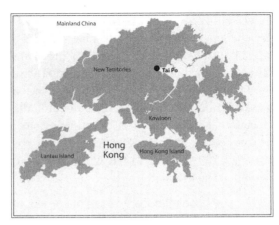

Map of Hong Kong

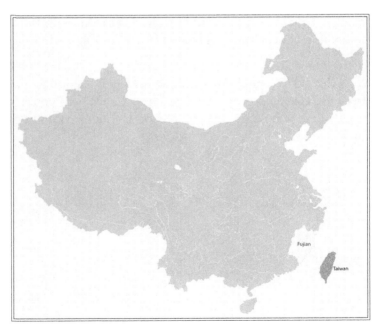

Map of Fujian

1

WE HAVE TO RUN!

Fujian Province, China, 2000

At 9:30 p.m., I arrived with some Chinese house church*
companions at a small home in Fuzhou, the capital city
of Fujian Province in China. I entered to see about fifteen
Chinese pastors inside, all women except for one man.**
Their faces lit up when they saw me, eager to receive
words of encouragement, prayers, and teaching.
They were all waiting to hear me preach, but I was
so tired and dirty from the exhausting travel. I asked if
I could shower first and then speak with them. It had
been two days since my last shower, and I was ready
to feel clean and refreshed before I shared God's
Word.

I turned to the house church sister who owned
the house, to ask for my China-issued "Home
Return Permit" and plane ticket back to Hong
Kong, which she had been holding for me.***
She went upstairs to retrieve my permit, and I took off
my shoes to enter the bathroom and take a shower
downstairs.

Suddenly I heard a voice cry out, "Teacher Barnabas,
we have to run!" I looked toward the front door as

---

* The Chinese House Church has been known by different names at different times, including "underground church," "underground house church," "persecuted church," and "house church movement." This book will refer to it as the 'house church movement" in most cases.

** Women pastors are common throughout China. There is a shortage of men in the Chinese House Church, as well as men who are willing to take leadership and pastoral positions. Countless women have filled this critical gap and placed themselves on the front lines of persecution. Without them, many house churches would simply not exist.

*** I had to apply for a Home Return Permit every time I entered China, and was required to carry it on me at all times. It was proof I could return to Hong Kong, and I had to show it to officers upon request.

three police officers forced open the front door and stormed in, just a few meters away from me.

We ran.

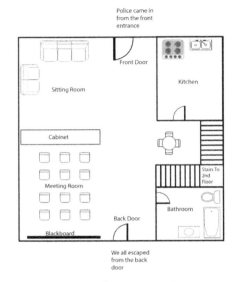

Floor plan of the house in Fujian

No time to grab anything. Not even shoes. I ran barefoot. Fortunately, there was a back door and gate that led to fields behind the house. I had so much adrenaline in that moment, that I think I ran fast enough to qualify for the Olympic 100-meter dash.

I raced into total darkness. I didn't know where I was, and I couldn't see anything around me. I had never been there before. I was a foreigner, a Hong Kong citizen, not yet familiar with China. I barely even spoke Mandarin at that point. I could hear the footsteps of police officers behind me, so I ran even faster.

But I wasn't scared. When I decided to serve the house churches in China, I knew someday this would happen.

I just didn't expect it so soon.

I had to run. Any kind of Christian gathering is not allowed in mainland China, outside of the strictly-controlled, government-run church, known as the Three-Self Church. China has been officially atheist since Mao Zedong consolidated control through his Communist Revolution in 1949. The initial stance of the Chinese Communist Party (CCP) at that time was to allow — but discourage — Christianity, as long as the people worshipped within the government-run Three-Self Church, and obeyed its strict, unbiblical rules. Christians who wanted to worship God without any government interference, and according to their conscience before God, took their churches "underground," forming what is now known as the Chinese House Church movement. The term "underground" referred largely to house churches that formed a network under the radar of local authorities, and outside of government approval. However, many of the churches were literally underground, painstakingly dug out by hand or small hand tools, often at night to avoid unwanted attention.

Chinese communism is a totalitarian system that exercises complete authority over the individual. There can be no higher authority than the government; therefore, there cannot be a God. Christianity, along with other religions, dilutes the authority of the state. Therefore, it must be crushed into oblivion. Unless I wanted to be crushed by the state, I had to run. I had to make it all the way back to my home, Hong Kong.

Hong Kong, 1956

My parents' small fishing boat rocked back and forth in the waves of the South China Sea off the coast of Hong Kong. It was June. The tropical air was hot and heavy. My father was a poor fisherman. He and my mother, along with my brothers and sisters, lived on the small fishing boat. Fishing was their livelihood, and the boat was their home. When my mother was in labor with me, there was no time to make it to a hospital on shore. She gave birth to me right there on the boat.

But I was born sick. By the time I was one year old, I had developed a serious heart problem. My parents had no money for doctors or medical treatment. They were sure I would die. My brother, who had been born a year before me, had died of the same sickness. Even if I lived, they had little means to feed me or provide an education.

My grandfather prayed desperately to God to heal me. He also made God a promise. He was attending a small fishing village church in Tai Po, and the pastor and his wife had no children. If I lived, my grandfather would ask my parents to let the pastor and wife of this small church raise me as their own child.

Miraculously, I was healed. My parents brought me, when I was two years old, to the pastor of the Tai Po church and his wife. At this time, the pastor was already seventy-one, and his wife was sixty-two, so they thought they were too old to raise a baby. However, my grandfather insisted, because he had made a promise to the Lord. With their agreement, my parents placed me into the arms of the pastor and his wife. My family went back to their fishing boat, and from that moment on, I was raised by this Christian couple.

The pastor and his wife led the Chinese Full Gospel Church, a charismatic church started by North American missionaries. Four of these churches were established along the coasts of Hong Kong, in little fishing and farming communities, and still exist to this day.

The pastor and his wife never slept together in the same room. The wife slept in one room and the pastor in another, both in the tiny upstairs of the church. I slept in the same room as the pastor, but he died three years after I was given to them. After that, the church took the room from us, and I had to sleep on a wooden church bench. I don't remember the pastor very well, and we didn't talk much. However,

I do remember he was kind to me. I don't remember him praying with me or teaching me much about anything, but I was also very quiet. It's not that I was unhappy, I just didn't talk much to anyone when I was young.

Wooden bench that I slept on as a child

I did have many questions. I wondered who my real family was, and where they were. Some of the women in the church secretly told me I was not the real son of the pastor. In fact, they said, my real father was a poor fisherman, and my family lived on a fishing boat with my many brothers and sisters. They warned me to keep this a secret, because my adoptive mother didn't want me to know. So I kept it all a secret. I didn't dare say a word. After my adoptive father died, my adoptive mother started beating me, almost every day. If she found out that I knew the truth, I knew she would beat me more. Even when I was a boy, I felt that some people's purpose in life was to make other people feel unpleasant. My childhood was often combative, and my adoptive mother and I fought every day. I was a boy with many questions, but few answers. She did not trust me because I was not her real son. She was always afraid that I would run away and not take care of her.

2
I FELT LIKE A SLAVE

Fujian, China, 2000

As I raced barefoot through the near-total darkness of an unknown Chinese countryside, with the police chasing after me, I realized I had no idea of the intensity of the political storm I had traveled directly into when I left Hong Kong only a few days earlier. I prayed as I ran for my life. I still remember my prayer, "Lord, please help me out! I do not know what to do, but You know. Please give me the strength I need. I do not want to be in prison in China, but if this is Your plan, please help me. I cannot even trust myself. I am afraid I may betray You if they beat me up. Give me the strength so that I will not betray You and the church. I need a miracle! Amen!" I repeated this prayer several times as I ran. Whenever people need to solve a problem, they often can call their friends or relatives to help, but I could only call Jesus. But believe me, when we pray, God can make things happen beyond our imagination.

––––––––––––––

It was October 2000, and the Chinese government was locked in a bitter dispute with the Vatican, the Hong Kong Catholic Church, and the Chinese underground Catholic Church in the Fujian Province of China.

The Catholic Church in Hong Kong was canonizing Chinese and foreign missionaries who had been killed in China between 1648 and 1930, which meant these martyrs were posthumously being officially declared as saints. Eighty-seven of them were Chinese Catholics and thirty-three were

European missionaries who were killed during various wars and rebellions, including the Opium Wars and the Boxer Rebellion. The Catholic Church considered them martyrs for the faith, but the Chinese government was campaigning vigorously against this action. They claimed the martyrs were guilty of "monstrous crimes against the Chinese people" and had "glorified Western imperialism." This belief was not new at all in China and had actually been held ever since the first Christian missionary arrived in China. Many indigenous people equated the conversion of one new Christian with the loss of one Chinese person. Furthermore, they viewed the coming of Christianity as the tool of Western aggression and the missionaries as pioneers.

After the Communist Revolution of 1949, Mao's Chinese Communist Party (CCP) could not tolerate a "Western" religion such as Christianity having any influence on Chinese culture, so Christianity was outlawed. Now, in 2000, China's answer to the impending "Western" canonization was a wave of arrests of Catholic leaders. China also began to ordain the CCP's own bishops into the CCP-controlled Catholic Church, known as the Patriotic Catholic Church Movement.

One of the 120 martyrs to be canonized was a Chinese bishop who had worked in Fujian Province, which is located on the coast of southeast China, directly west of Taiwan. As a result, the underground Catholic house church in Fujian Province had held many celebrations, right before I arrived to meet with the Protestant house churches. Before my arrival, the police had arrested at least twenty-three foreigners in Fujian, and they were looking for more. However, I knew little of these details before I traveled into China.

———————————

It was late October when I flew from Hong Kong to Beijing, and then on to Datong in Shanxi Province, where I worked several days training and interviewing house church pastors. On Monday, October 23, I flew to Fuzhou, the capital of Fujian, with my friend Sun, one of the young men who often traveled with me as a local guide.

We landed in Fuzhou, and four female house church pastors greeted us at the airport. They knew the city of Fuzhou, and would help us travel undetected to different house churches and meetings. But before we left the airport, I needed to buy my return ticket to Hong Kong. I went to the ticketing counter, but was told if I bought the ticket in the city, rather than the airport, I would save a significant amount of money. Since we would be traveling through the main city, I agreed to wait and buy my ticket when we drove through.

I didn't like traveling without a return ticket, but I can't always know my exact travel plans until I meet with the pastors. I never went into China unprepared. I always kept my Home Return Permit and tickets (plane, bus, or train) with me at all times. I never knew when the secret police would come through my door, or catch me without my permit. My unease grew worse when our schedule changed, as often happens in China, and we bypassed Fuzhou on the way to the house churches. I would have to wait until Thursday morning, the day of my return flight, to buy my ticket.

————————————

The conflict brewing in China was an essential part of communism. Communism begins with conflict—the conflict between different classes of society and people groups. The CCP is all about power struggles. Revolution starts and ends through power struggles. There is a saying in China, "Do not be stupid; use your power before it expires!" The conflict bred by the Chinese government pitted neighbor against neighbor, and children against parents. The result was a pervasive culture of fear and lying, even when it was unnecessary.

Many times, when I'm with Chinese pastors, I hear the same conversation when they answer the phone:

> *"Ni hao (Hello), this is Jing. Sorry, I am in a meeting in Shanghai now! I'll call you back later today!"*

After the pastor hangs up the phone, I ask him:

> *"You are in Beijing, why did you say you are in Shanghai!"*

> *"Oh, I do not want him to know where I am, so I just made up a place and said Shanghai!"*

> *"Brother, what you just said is lying! You're in Beijing, not in Shanghai! Just tell him you can't reveal where you are or that it is not convenient to tell him!"*

> *"Yes, thank you for your advice. It is very common in China for us to lie. It affects all of us, including me, a pastor. I will be more careful in what I say! We need to live out a good testimony! Lying is not good, even with a good intention!"*

China has its own cultural practices that are very different from the rest of the world. In 2006, on a hot summer day, I was sitting in the first-class lounge at Wuhan airport. At that time, Wuhan airport was not big, and I was upgraded by Air China to fly first class to Beijing.

It was an early morning flight. The lounge was small, and almost no one was there, except me and one other man, who was talking quietly on the phone. Suddenly, he raised his voice, so loudly that even people outside the lounge could hear him.

> *"No, you cannot make the change! We just signed the contract in your office yesterday afternoon! A valid contract needs to be signed by both parties, and even if I consent to your change, I need to sign the contract, but I cannot! I'm on my way to Beijing and connecting to my flight back to Singapore. I have to attend some important meetings when I'm back, and the most important thing is*

that I do not agree with you!"

He listened for a moment and then replied,

"Well, I know you are the boss and represent the government, but a contract is a contract. It took us three months to come to this agreement and sign the contract yesterday. You cannot change it overnight! I cannot make this decision, so you'll have to talk to my boss in Singapore!"

After he hung up his cell phone, he looked at me and said,

"You do not look like mainland Chinese. Sorry I spoke too loudly, but I think you can understand my frustration in doing business with the Chinese, especially the Chinese government!"

I just smiled and nodded my head. I didn't want to discuss this because we were in China, and there are eyes and ears everywhere in China, always watching and listening. If we said something the government didn't like, we could be reported.

In Chinese culture, an important part of communication is listening to what is not said. The Chinese call this "implication." Words have endless levels of meaning. Consider the following example:

Person 1:

"Thank you so much for coming to the meeting. We had a great meeting today. Where shall we go for dinner?"

Person 2:

"It doesn't matter. You know me, I like all kinds of food."

Person 1:

"Good, let's go out for a steak dinner. There is a great Western restaurant close by!"

Person 2:

"Oh, I just remembered that I must go home early today. I am sorry, let's have dinner next time we meet."

The man made an excuse because he does not like steak. However, he will not express this or ask for a different restaurant. He will find an excuse to leave. The implication, or unspoken words, here may also suggest that he does not feel the meeting went as well as the other person thinks.

When I studied the history of China in high school, I learned that the 5,000 years of Chinese history have been 5,000 years of corruption. China does not have any morals or ethics that remain to be corrupted. One of the founders of the Chinese Communist Party, Chen Duxiu 陳獨秀, once said that the spirit of Jesus, which is love, is not in the Communist Party. But I say that China does need Jesus.

China is full of intentionally sown conflict and distrust. But I was no stranger to conflict. I knew it well from my early childhood and how damaging it was.

Hong Kong, 1960s

As I mentioned a few pages back, my adoptive father passed away when I was five years old, and when I was twelve years old, the Hong Kong government legalized my adoption.

On my adoptive father's seventy-fifth birthday, many of his friends and church members came to celebrate and enjoy a big meal. At this time, there was a woman who had become like a daughter to my adoptive parents and a sister to me, even though she was thirty years older than I was.* She lived next to the church, and had married a man from mainland China who was much older than she was, and had previously been married. His first wife had an eighteen-year-old son who had escaped China by swimming to Hong Kong from Guangdong Province (which was common in those times), only two days prior to my adoptive father's birthday.

---

* This girl was like a goddaughter to them, although they had not legally adopted her. Chinese culture demands that relationships exist between people who are close to the people who are close to you, therefore, she was like a godsister to me.

He was now living with them in their tiny single room.

This new arrangement made my sister very upset, because she already had three children with her husband, and now she was saddled with the adult child of her husband's former wife. She refused to let him come to my adoptive father's birthday party. My adoptive father was a kind man, however, and wanted this young man, who had just escaped China, to come to his party.

At first there was no sign of the young man, but halfway through the meal, he walked in. My sister was furious. My father tried to calm her down, and insisted he could stay. But she turned her anger on him, screaming that if he wanted the young man to stay, then she would leave and never return. He would be dead to her.

My father suddenly fell to the floor and didn't move. An ambulance finally arrived and took him to the hospital. The next morning, he was pronounced dead from a heart attack.

After my adoptive father passed away, life was difficult. My adoptive mother was already sixty-six years old and physically frail. She had difficulty with her eyesight and walked very slowly. At five years old, I began working as the church janitor, and would even go out for more work to make money. As the janitor, I did everything. I cleaned the toilets and mopped the floors. I changed the light bulbs, getting electric shocks in the process, because I had no training and didn't know what I was doing.

I would also rise early in the morning to assemble, sell, and distribute newspapers. (I had stacks of individual newspaper sheets from multiple Hong Kong newspapers. I had to assemble each newspaper carefully in the correct order by hand before I could sell and deliver them.) I would then go home to make plastic flowers. The wealthiest man in Hong Kong, at the time, had made his first billion dollars by selling plastic flowers to the United States. I hoped to make money and have a future like him, but I was only one boy, who made and sold what I could. On weekends, especially on Saturdays, I would work a full day in the wet market, helping the vendors with different tasks to make some money.

Even though I was only a child, I was the one taking care of my adoptive mother, not the other way around. I worked and provided for her needs, but she never showed me love in return. Instead, she abused me every day. In those days, it was common for parents in Hong Kong to abuse their children when they were angry, but that didn't make it easy for me to accept it. I wasn't doing anything to deserve her abuse. She would tell her friends and church members that she was giving me money for school and that she spent a lot of money on me every month, but it was all lies. I had nothing and often went hungry.

For five years, I ate one meal per day, dinner, because my adoptive mother didn't give me any money to buy food. Dinner was usually water and some leftovers, even if I was doing the cooking for her, but no one knew my difficulties. A few times, my mother gave me enough coins to buy a small piece of bread. But often I was so hungry that I would sometimes steal money from the newspaper stand where I sold newspapers.

Starving as a growing young boy is very difficult. That's why now, even if I don't want to eat, I eat because I don't want to be starving again. I really praise the Lord for my good physical health. I never had any problems with my health, even after eating only one meal a day for five years, when my body was growing and needed nutrition. The whole time my mother continued to lie and tell others that I had everything I needed. To me, it is a miracle how God sustained me.

When I wasn't working, I also attended school and completed my homework. In addition, I had to take care of my adoptive mother. I had to wake her up, put toothpaste on her toothbrush, make hot water for her tea, fill a plastic basin with warm water, and place her towel next to the basin so she could wash her face. I felt like a slave. At this time, my godsister, her husband,

and their three sons were also living next to us. Many times, I was forced to cook for the entire family and wash their dishes after they ate.

3
FORCED TO STEAL

Fujian, China, 2000

After Sun and I left the airport, accompanied by the four house church sisters, we drove to a house where we planned to stay Monday night. We would travel on Tuesday, then return on Wednesday night before my Thursday flight back to Hong Kong.

Fuzhou was known as a city of women, which was why the four house church sisters were traveling with us. Most of the men in the city had fled China. They had illegally entered the United States, Germany, and Japan, and they worked to send money back to support their families. They would usually only return after ten or fifteen years, which meant that the husband and wife would be separated for a long time. The women would stay home to raise their children and take care of their elders. Out of all the places I visited in Fuzhou, I only met four men between the ages of twenty and forty-five.

Another unique aspect of Fuzhou was the safety that house churches experienced there. Everyone from Datong, Beijing, and Fuzhou kept telling me that Fujian Province was safe for underground churches, because they had built a close relationship with the government-run church, the Three-Self Patriotic Movement (TSPM).

Although the TSPM was initiated by the CCP, it was later eradicated in 1966 during the Cultural Revolution. Concerning Christianity, Mao dictated a change in strategy, from containment to elimination. Chairman Mao proudly proclaimed a eulogy for the death of Christianity in China, saying, "It is dead, and the yoke of imperialistic religions is broken once and for all; even the memories are destroyed." Mao's wife, Jiang Qing, made the famous statement, "Christianity in China has been confined to the history section of the museum. It is dead and buried. And there is only one Bible in China; it is in the museum in Beijing."*

The government ended all Three-Self Church activities, and began a vicious campaign to eliminate all house churches as well. Imprisonment, brutal interrogation, and even execution were all a reality for Christians, whose only crime was being faithful and obedient to Jesus Christ. Known Chinese Christians were often fired from their jobs, expelled from schools, stripped of material possessions, publicly humiliated, and tortured. They endured inhumane conditions in hard labor camps, where their thinking was to be "reformed." They were falsely accused as American spies, counterrevolutionaries, and criminals, and they were rejected by their fellow Chinese neighbors and even family members. It was impossible to flee persecution and establish churches elsewhere, because China enforced "residential registration," which officially identified a person as a citizen of a specific area, and restricted him or her from moving about or going abroad.

In 1979, the Three-Self Church was re-instated under China's "Open Door Policy," which increased the personal freedoms and opportunities for Chinese citizens. However, it was still tightly controlled. Therefore, many Chinese Christians refused to attend the Three-Self Church, and instead still met in house churches. Fortunately, they experienced less persecution than before.

The "Three-Self" in Three-Self churches stands for self-governance, self-support, and self-propagation. Three-Self churches are required to reject all foreign influence and display "patriotic" loyalty to China. What is important to understand is

---

* I saw Chairman Mao's wife, Jiang Qing, say this on a TV broadcast to Hong Kong when I was a child.

that the CCP (Chinese Communist Party) is the absolute head and authority of the Three-Self Church. In China, it is often said, "The government is the head of the Three-Self Patriotic Movement. God is the head of the House Church movement." The CCP decides how many people can be baptized, who is allowed to preach, and what is to be preached. Preaching on the resurrection of Jesus Christ, the basis upon which the truth of Christianity rests, is forbidden in some provinces, as well as any preaching about the return of Jesus Christ. Jesus' resurrection and second coming directly contradict the ultimate authority of the CCP. Evangelism, as well as importing or printing Bibles, is forbidden. Bibles distributed by the TSPM are strictly controlled. Christians are required to register all Bibles with the government, which has created a government registry of Chinese Christians. Of course, China is a big country, so the registry may not be enforced in some locations. Government officials, soldiers, teachers, and minors cannot be Christians or attend Three-Self Church services.[vii]

The Three-Self Church is not allowed to focus on the truth of the gospel. Rather, it must focus on the ethical teachings of Jesus, such as love and non-violence, as it benefits Chinese society. The Three-Self Church is a tool of indoctrination and propaganda for the CCP. God-ordained precepts like "love thy neighbor," and "obey government authorities," are key principles used to enforce unquestioning loyalty to the Chinese government. In places like China, and now Hong Kong, those who question or challenge the authorities are considered reactionary and disrespectful. Their voices will be wiped out, and they will disappear. Resistance is even more self-defeating.

When I visited Fuzhou in 2000, Fujian was the only province where the government allowed house church pastors to run authorized church activities. But this also meant that many of the house churches had to register with the TSPM. Some of the Three-Self Church pastors were tasked with controlling the house churches and suppressing them if they evangelized too much, worked outside of their respective towns or villages, or broke other government-imposed rules.

This kind of situation was rare in China, but it happened in Fujian Province. Therefore, everyone considered Fujian a safe place for public Christian worship, as well as for visiting foreigners like me. While I was aware of problems and divisions within the church, I wasn't fully aware of how drastically the situation had changed in Fujian, regarding the disagreement with the Catholic Church.

Sun and I left early on Tuesday morning to travel to the town of Fuqing. We arrived at a small home at 8:45 a.m. and immediately started training until the evening.

This is very common in China. Chinese Bible trainings are not Western-style conferences with comfortable rooms, chairs, and snacks. Trainings are held in small, packed rooms or even in underground caves. There is no air conditioning in the summer, and if there is heat in the winter, it is provided by a simple wood-burning stove. Sometime the only light comes from a single light bulb hanging from a wire in the middle of the room. Sessions start early and go as late as possible with only a few short breaks. Often, people sit on the ground, either due to a lack of chairs, or to save space so everyone can fit inside. The only toilets are unenclosed holes in the ground, offering no privacy.

These men and women were hungry to learn the Word of God. Persecution had not diluted the church as the Chinese government hoped. Instead, it had the opposite effect, and distilled the church down to those who were dedicated in their faith. They risked imprisonment to preach the gospel and share Christ with anyone God put before them. This was very different from the Christianity lived out in the small fishing village church in which I was raised.

Hong Kong, 1960s

My church in the fishing village, along with three other small churches in Hong Kong, had been planted by a charismatic North American missionary. These four churches were located in the fishing villages of Tai Po, Stanley, Sai Kung, and Tap Mun. Tap Mun is now called Grass Island, a small outlying island used mostly by fishermen to park their boats. When my adoptive father passed away, the church in Tai Po felt my mother could not take over as pastor, because she could not write at all, and could only read a little Chinese. She had no theological training, and could not preach the way the church wanted. The church also did not tithe, so they did not have any money to hire another pastor. It was decided my mother and I could stay at the church if we worked as janitors. They would have guest speakers preach every Sunday for free. My adoptive father had helped to plant the church, which made some people respect him. If they did not take care of my adoptive mother (she was sixty-five years old then and could not make a living), what could she do? So the church gave her a stipend every month, and let us stay at the church for free. Because my adoptive mother made me do all the work, I was the sole church janitor. All this time, she verbally and physically abused me. I grew angry, resentful, and even hateful of women, because I thought they were all like my mother.

Meanwhile, the unfaithful church deacons allowed every kind of false pastor through the front doors. These so-called "preachers" would sell fake Chinese medicine to the poor and uneducated church members. Some would lay a stack of handkerchiefs, which they had prayed over, on the pulpit. For a donation, church members could take a handkerchief and place it under their pillow, or the pillow of someone who was sick, in order for them to be healed.

There was no biblical teaching at the church. Some of the pastors who came said that everyone who was a Christian must speak in tongues. Even though I was young, I didn't believe that was true. I read the Bible myself, and knew it was a spiritual gift some had, but not everyone. In fact, one Chinese couple came and claimed to be pastors, but I later learned the husband was just a businessman from Hong Kong Island. They had helped the missionary to found these four churches, and because the wife could speak English, they acted like they had authority. I do not know how well she spoke English, because I did not know much English at the time. When I was five, the North American missionary came to visit once every two to three years. He was not living in Hong Kong and could not speak our language. When I was around eight years old, I did not see him anymore, so I presume he may have died.

The couple used to come once every two months to lead communion. They dressed nicely when they came to see us, even though we were poor and only had old, used clothing to wear. Each time they came, they didn't speak to anyone—no hellos or greetings. They would enter the church, walk right up to the podium, kneel down, and begin praying in tongues. I still remember how every time they spoke, it was the same language and the same words, just repeated over and over. As a young boy, I found it interesting, but it also formed my first impressions of Christians—that many of them were hypocrites. It looked very spiritual when they were up at the podium praying like that, but afterward, I saw how badly they spoke to people and treated them.

By the time I was seven, my thinking was quite mature, because I had to make all kinds of decisions every day for myself. I swore I would never be a Christian. The people around me were hypocrites. My adoptive mother was abusive and unethical. The people in the church, including the deacons, did not behave as sincere Christians. Whenever the Salvation Army donated relief items to our village, they would force me to steal some, and then sell them at the market to earn money. I would sell rice, canned meats like spam, cooking oil, and other items meant to help the hungry of the church. I was allowed to keep the donated clothes, only because we couldn't sell those. They were all Western clothes with Western sizing, which doesn't fit Asians properly. So I grew up wearing used, oddly fitting clothes my entire childhood. I didn't have a single new piece of clothing until I was sixteen years old.

I was also forced to steal rice from the church to sell at the market. I had to be more careful about this, because there were many people around. However, I had a method that was never discovered. I had a small bag and a bamboo stick, sharpened on one end. I would take the bags of rice stored at the church—donated to feed the needy—and pierce the bottom of each bag. Because the bamboo stick was hollow, the rice would flow through it into my smaller bag. The bags looked undamaged from the top, and because I took only a small amount from each one, they still looked full. There were also many mice in the church, which were blamed for any holes in the bags. I did that for more than three years, under the orders of my mother and the church deacons.

Rice sacks that I used to steal from

They would even follow me to the market, to make sure I gave them all the money made from the stolen rice and other goods. I knew stealing was wrong, but they made me steal. Even when I was young, I had the ability to distinguish right from wrong. I promised myself I would never be a Christian, because I would hold myself to a higher moral standard than they did.

But my eyes were not on Jesus at the time. They were on other people and their faults. I wasn't saved, so I wasn't thinking spiritually about these things. I was a boy, and based on their actions, I decided not to believe in Jesus, or have anything to do with God.

Even after I became a Christian, I would still look at other people's lives and think that Jesus was not fair. I judged other's hearts without knowing Jesus' will or His heart, sometimes forgetting He is bigger than I am. It took time to overcome this way of thinking that began in me at such a young, impressionable age. Yet in time, He taught me it doesn't matter how good or bad people are. What matters is that Jesus Christ is Lord. Therefore, I should look only to Him, trust Him, and hold myself accountable to Him.

4

TOLD TO PREACH

FUJIAN, CHINA, 2000

It was late in the evening when Sun and I finished training in Fuqing (福清). We took a bus to another town farther east, very close to the east coast, where I preached for two hours at another house church. No matter where I was, I was never far from a house church, regardless of its size or meeting place.

China's house church movements are vast networks that permeate every corner of China's sprawling geography and include an estimated 110–150 million Christians, although an exact number is impossible to know. Chinese believers have been meeting in homes since the turn of the twentieth century, but at that time, they rarely used the term "house church," opting instead for the expression "home meetings." While the degree of political consciousness varied across home meetings after the 1949 revolution, all groups shared the belief that human authorities had no right to dictate how God should be worshipped. They regarded the TSPM as theologically unorthodox and spiritually weak, and they rejected it as a propaganda tool of the CCP. Christians who wanted to continue their meetings could only do so secretly at home in underground churches, later referred to as "house churches."

In 1958, Chairman Mao introduced the Great Leap Forward campaign (1958–1962) to transform China's agricultural economy into a modern communist society, with high national production through industrialization and collectivization. In order to accomplish this, the Chinese authorities seized many TSPM church buildings and used them as factories, schools, and government offices.

This horrific period resulted in the largest famine in world history, with an estimated 18–45 million deaths. It forced many believers who attended Three-Self churches into the House Church movement. When the TSPM began in 1952, Wang Ming-Dao 王明道 and Watchman Nee 倪柝聲 became the most influential leaders of the house churches. These men criticized the leaders of the Three-Self churches as betrayers of their Lord. Consequently, the Chinese government persecuted Wang and Nee, labeled them as counterrevolutionaries, threw them into prison, and shut down their churches. A second generation of leaders, however, rose up to take their place. Later, in the 1960s and 1970s, these leaders were also put into prison. Most of them spent more than twenty years in prison for the gospel. These leaders include Samuel Lamb 林獻羔, Allen Yuan 袁相枕, Epaphras of China (Weizun Wu) 中國的以巴弗吳維樽, Musheng Li 李天恩 (慕聖), Moshan Xie 謝模善, and many others.

During the Cultural Revolution (1966–1976), persecution of the underground church became widespread. Authorities caught house church leaders, beat them, and put them into prison. Although many believers were dispersed and left without leaders, certain laypeople strongly believed that Christians should continue to meet together. Lay leaders accepted the responsibility to connect with other believers and pastor them during this difficult time. To avoid detection by the authorities, believers met in remote or hidden locations at night. Their simple gatherings included Bible reading, a sermon, sharing with those in need, and praying for one another. Believers across China carefully hid the Word of God in the ground — sometimes in coffins — in order to safeguard it. If the authorities caught and imprisoned a leader, another believer rose up to take over his duties, while others in the church supported the family of the imprisoned. In this time of darkness, the message of eternal hope provided encouragement to the church. Through the house churches, the church grew in faith and numbers all across China.

The House Church is a mighty force—one the communist regime has tried to contain. The widespread persecution has inevitably caused the House Church to expand as believers are forced to find new places and ways to meet together. It trains them to effectively lead others to Christ. This creative approach to ministry has produced six major networks, or movements, that range in size from 5–10 million Christians each, with many smaller regional networks of up to half a million believers respectively. Smaller house church movements may be located in only one or two of China's twenty-three provinces and various regions, while larger movements stretch across the entire nation.

After I finished preaching in the house church in Fuqing, our group needed to split up. The house church sisters needed to travel back to the main city of Fuzhou, while Sun and I needed to travel farther east to a small island off the coast. The sisters offered to buy my plane ticket for me when they arrived in Fuzhou, so that I would be sure to have it for the Thursday flight back to Hong Kong. The flight was popular, and might be fully booked before I would be back to buy it myself. I hesitated, because this meant I would need to give them my Home Return Permit. I knew I should never be without my permit. Everywhere I went in China, I always kept my money, Home Return Permit, and Hong Kong ID with me at all times, even in the bathroom when I took a shower. I wore a vest with many pockets to ensure I never lost them. But the sisters assured me it would be fine, and the thought of missing the Thursday flight overruled my hesitation. So I made the biggest mistake of the trip and gave them my permit.

We parted ways, and Sun and I drove to the coast and boarded a boat to go to a small island with a new house church. We arrived on the island late Tuesday night. This island is the part of China that lies closest to Taiwan, at only about 110 miles away from the Taiwanese coast. After interviewing and preaching, I was exhausted and ready to sleep. As I went to the room where I would sleep, one pastor said to me, "Brother Barnabas, when you wake up in the morning, don't go outside. The island is crawling with army troops because of the situation in Taiwan. Many foreigners have been arrested, and you will stick out as a foreigner." This was not the news I wanted to hear before I went to sleep. But I was well aware of the conflict between Taiwan and China, which has existed since at least 1949.

The founding of the Republic of China in 1912 ended 4,000 years of imperial rule in China. Later, in 1928, the Republic was unified under the "Kuomintang," or Chinese Nationalist Party. However, the Kuomintang was weakened by the end of the Second Sino-Japanese War (1937–1945). Conflicts with the CCP, in existence since 1920, intensified. This led to the Chinese Civil War, which lasted from 1945 to 1949. The Kuomintang and the capital city of Nanjing fell to the CCP's People Liberation Army in 1949, after which the Kuomintang fled to the island of Taiwan, which was then controlled by the Japanese. They took with them several hundred thousand military troops, approximately two million refugees, gold reserves, and Chinese cultural treasures.

After the Japanese surrendered at the end of World War II, the Republic of China was officially established on Taiwan. By contrast, Chairman Mao Zedong formed the *People's* Republic of China on the mainland. Both countries insisted—and still insist—they are the only one true China. The People's Republic of China is adamant it will rule and integrate Taiwan, even by force.

In the year 2000, Taiwan had just completed its second presidential election, during which time China had saber-rattled. The election of a new leader in Taiwan brought to power a party that emphasized Taiwan's independence from China.

With all this in mind, I asked if I should leave the island that night, but they said it would be fine if I stayed downstairs and waited until the next day to leave. Traveling and training had been long and tiring. I fell asleep quickly, even as my mind wandered to the political conflicts of China I had read about as a young boy selling newspapers.

HONG KONG, 1970s

When I was six and delivering newspapers every morning starting at 5 a.m., I had the opportunity to read many different newspapers. By the time I was seven years old, I had learned enough Chinese characters to understand the newspapers and think about what was happening in China and the world. Even at this young age as an unsaved boy, God allowed me to share in the hardships and sufferings of Christians in China. I began to observe the society around me: the politics, leaders, and institutions. Many people in Hong Kong praised China and Chairman Mao, but I asked myself many questions and began to think critically through these issues.

I would go to bookstores to read the books that I didn't have money to buy. I would also go to the library. My mother never taught me anything. I had to teach myself about these things, and I was hungry to learn. I saw people swimming to Hong Kong to escape from China, and I knew things must be very bad there. I thought, "If China is so good and wonderful, why do so many Chinese citizens risk everything by attempting to swim and sneak into Hong Kong every day?" Yes, every day! Little was known about the true political and economic state of China at the time, and CCP propaganda was rampant. Nevertheless, I was determined to discover the truth.

I hated Chairman Mao and the pain he inflicted on people. I hated him so much that I wrote an essay in school that I wanted to kill Chairman Mao when I was nine or ten years old! My teacher called me into his room and explained that I could never write that again. If I did, I would be in serious trouble. At the time, I was the top student and a leader in my class, so I had to be careful not to destroy my future academic opportunities. Yes, Hong Kong was still under British rule at the time, but China was intent on taking over Hong Kong and China's influence was steadily increasing.

For five years, when I was in middle school and high school, I went to school in Kowloon, which is the mainland side of Hong Kong. I did very well as a student, which gave me the opportunity to go to the top secondary school in Hong Kong. Even at the age of seven, I was one of the few members of my church who had any education. I began to read the Bible for the church prayer meetings. When I was thirteen, the church deacons asked me to teach Sunday school to my peers. One Sunday, when I was fourteen, we had no guest pastor to preach. We sang for an hour, but no one ever showed up. The deacons pointed to me and asked me to stand up and preach! At the age of fourteen, I preached my first sermon. I wasn't even a Christian, yet I stood up and gave a forty-five-minute sermon without any preparation because I could read and knew the Bible.

The children of fishermen were rarely educated. If children live and work on a boat every day, then they have no school nearby to attend. The Hong Kong government built some schools specifically for the children of fishermen, but even then, most children could only go one or two days a week. My real mother and father had many children. I had two older sisters, one older brother, two younger sisters, and two younger brothers. If my parents had not given me away, I would have had no chance of an education.

I'm glad that God had a special plan for me as a fisherman's son. If I had lived on the boat with my family, I probably would have been in the same situation as all my sisters and brothers, who received little-to-no education. But because I was adopted, not only did I go to school, but I also finished high school when I was fifteen years old. Even though I worked multiple jobs while I was in school, I was still able to be a great student. I didn't have much time to study, but God gave me a great memory, almost photographic, which allowed me to always be the top student in my class.

After I graduated high school at age fifteen, I wanted to continue my education. I attended evening classes for two years, which allowed me to be accepted into the University of Hong Kong. I believed at that rate, I could earn one or two PhDs before I was thirty years old, which I wanted. However, my adoptive mother wanted me to work and go to a technical school instead, so I could learn a trade and keep earning money for her. So I enrolled at Kowloon Technical School and learned woodworking, metalwork, as well as mathematics, advanced mathematics, Chinese literature and history, social studies, health studies, geography, technical drawing, English language, and other subjects.

Now I understand God was teaching me spiritual lessons. While I was caring for my abusive mother and waiting to attend university, God was developing my character so He could use me and I could serve Him. Had I gone to university, I know I would have placed too much confidence in my knowledge and myself. I would have thought I was capable of anything, not needing to trust God for everything. I would have been successful and taken the glory for myself. Instead, God gave me the opportunity to be a student of Him, to use me for His glory.

I am amazed how our Lord loves every one of us and treats us equally. I was born on the South China Sea in a fishing boat, a fisherman's son. But God gave my brothers, sisters, and me the same wisdom as those who were born into good families. I don't believe in "blue bloods" or that if an intellectual marries another intellectual, they'll give birth to a highly intellectual baby. I'm a fisherman, and God has given me a good memory and wisdom like many other people. God is fair, and He takes good care of me.

I know that other than my adoptive parents and biological parents, I have our Lord as my heavenly Father. He loves and cares for me. I've been under His protection and His plan since I was born, and I will continue to do my best to serve Him and to be obedient to Him. Wherever He wants me to go, I will go.

When I grew up, it seemed I had nothing. I didn't know for sure who my parents were until after high school, but I knew God was with me. After I became a Christian, I knew I only needed one thing—the love of my Lord. With Him, everything is possible. It seems I have nothing, but I have His mercy and grace always with me, and I have His provision whenever He thinks I need it.

5

SURPRISED BY LOVE

FUJIAN, CHINA, 2000

The next morning on the island, we woke up and drove to the ferry that would take us back to the mainland. There were around thirty people on the ferry. I had my backpack with my clothes, computer, camera, and other items in it. But my backpack didn't look like the kind of backpacks in mainland China. It looked like the backpack of a foreigner. One of the pastors wanted to be helpful and took it to put it on his back. I protested, not wanting my backpack to draw attention to him, but it was impossible to argue because he was intent on helping me. After he took my backpack, he walked to the upper deck of the ferry to sit with Sun, while I stayed on the lower deck. Sun and the pastor saw three police officers on the upper deck, but it was too late to stand up and move. They didn't want to raise their suspicions. Unfortunately, the officers noticed the strange backpack and asked the pastor if the backpack was his and what was in it. Meanwhile, I had no idea any of this was happening.

The pastor was able to talk his way out of opening it for the police or admitting it was mine. As soon as the ferry reached the dock, the pastor jumped on his motorcycle with Sun and took off. They couldn't risk waiting for us because it possibly would have exposed all of us. Three pastors had stayed on the lower deck with me, so I remained with them. We didn't find out what had happened to Sun and the pastor until later that day.

The three pastors and I boarded a bus traveling back to Fuqing. We knew something bad had happened on the ferry, but we weren't sure what. We also noticed two secret police on the bus with us, so I knew we had to be alert.

In China, there are police officers who wear uniforms and handle standard community policing, but there are also secret police who wield wide-ranging powers. Their name, "secret police" is not a nickname either. The secret police agency of the People's Republic of China is part of the Ministry of State Security (MSS) in China and is responsible for spying on citizens, rooting out "dissidents," rounding them up for interrogation, and even worse, potentially making them disappear completely. Christians are considered dissidents.

CCP officials and secret police watch every village, every housing complex, and every factory to report any "abnormalities"—such as the presence of foreigners or an unusual volume of traffic in and out of certain buildings by unknown individuals. Any local house churches and training centers known to government officials are under constant surveillance. As a form of harassment, police frequently telephone pastors in order to track their movements and visit their churches on a regular basis.

When you're in China, you cannot talk about Jesus openly in any public places with a group of people. If it's one-on-one, it might be fine, but the secret police might still be listening. You cannot talk when you are walking on the city street. Your hotel room phones might be tapped. You cannot pray over a meal in public because they may be watching. When you're at home, they might call you to come to the local station to "have tea." This is their way of demanding you to come for an interrogation. You might leave . . . you might not.

China has hundreds of thousands of secret police who spread

out not only across China, but also within countries of interest to China. Now, in a new age of unparalleled technological advancement, China has become one of the most, if not the most, intrusive police states in the world. Advanced facial recognition cameras blanket all of China, including forced installations inside authorized churches. An estimated 600 million of these cameras are currently being installed across China. All messaging apps are monitored, along with captured voice samples for phone tapping recognition. In some provinces, government-mandated GPS trackers are installed on cars, and citizens are forced to undergo iris scans and DNA collection.

In the most tightly controlled provinces, armies of recruited civilians are paid to monitor groups of assigned houses and report everything to local authorities, even the occupants' political and religious beliefs. Citizens are forced to hand over their cellphones at mandatory police checkpoints, where the phones are plugged into computers that download all digital content including texts, emails, and photos. All of this has culminated in a "social credit system" where the slightest infractions are recorded, such as spreading gossip, jaywalking, or accumulating too much debt. This can result in people having their passport seized, being banned from plane or train travel, and losing higher education opportunities for their children. Their property can be seized, and their movements restricted, meaning they cannot leave their own city.

Even in 2000, before the advent of many of these technologies in mainland China, we had to stay alert. Despite the dangers, the pastors with me that day in Fujian, as well as others I have known, fear God more than they fear the government. For Christ, they are willing to risk their freedoms in a way none of us could have imagined before we were saved.

Hong Kong, 1970s

At the age of fifteen, I wanted nothing to do with Christ. I knew the Bible. I also knew the church. But what I had witnessed and experienced growing up caused me to not want any part of it. I wanted to focus on my education and work toward having a prosperous life.

I graduated high school at fifteen years old. I was young, but I was also eager to continue my education and begin university. My plan was to study for two more years and prepare for the university entrance exams. However, my adoptive mother said I needed to work and earn money for the family. It was difficult for me to find full-time work, but I took odd jobs delivering newspapers, making plastic flowers for factories to ship to the U.S., knitting sweaters with a simple machine, walking four miles on the railway track to check for cracks at night, working in the wet markets, and any other work I could find. I was too young to work a full-time job. Therefore, I had to find many small, part-time jobs that employers were willing to give a young boy.

As summer approached, a friend asked if I wanted to go to a summer camp with him. I didn't have the money to attend the camp. But he told me not to worry about the cost; it would be free for me. I knew it was a Christian camp, so I was sure it would be boring. However, it would be a nice break from my work. Because it was free, my adoptive mother would have one less reason to say no.

In fact, she was one reason I wanted to go to the camp. She was an angry woman who yelled at me, used me as her personal servant, and physically beat me. I never felt a mother's love from her. Never a hug. Never a kiss. Camp would be an escape from her, even if for a short time.

She said no. Even if the camp were free, she said, I would lose a week of income from not working. Later, she changed her mind. She knew I had worked hard for so many years, and a few days would be a good break for me.

For Westerners, summer camps mean acres of cabins, green grass and woods, lakes with canoes, swimming, sunshine, and endless games. But when I arrived at a small two-story building in Kowloon Tong that housed 120 youth, of which I was the youngest, there was no place for games or recreational activities. Every day was Bible study, preaching, and then one-on-one evangelism . . . and I wasn't even a Christian! I was so bored that I couldn't even pay attention. My mind would drift off into daydreaming. I didn't care about their Jesus or their Bible. I didn't want to be a Christian. I grew up in church and knew they were all hypocrites! In the one-on-one sessions, the counselor would tell me about Christ, but I knew how to avoid the conversation and not even make eye contact. There were others like me too. About one-third of the 120 youth were non-believers who had been invited by the Christian campers.

Like many summer camps, the last night was a special candlelight meeting, in which those who had accepted Christ could stand up and share their testimony. As these new Christians stood up and spoke, I was very happy because I had no reason to speak. I didn't enjoy speaking in public.

As I sat there, a pastor stood and quoted John 3:16, speaking of how God so loved the entire world. There was no lightning or thunder, and no beams of lights into the room. But in that instant, my heart and mind were filled with God's love for me, the conviction of my sin, and my need for Him as my Savior. The Holy Spirit entered my heart and turned it upside down.

I didn't speak in tongues, and only those closest to me could see the tears in my eyes as I silently repented and asked for forgiveness. I had read John 3:16 so many times before, and even preached on it when I was fourteen years old, but in that moment, it finally clicked. God changed my heart, my mind, and my beliefs. I went from a proud, defiant rebel to a humbled sinner, saved by grace.

I stood up and shared my testimony, tears of joy streaming down my face. I finally knew love, the ultimate love. I had never known love from my real mother, and never from my adoptive mother. As a little boy growing up, I want to be loved, but I didn't have a mother who would hold me in her arms. She never even trusted me. I knew that because she told me. But when the Holy Spirit came into my heart that night, it felt like God was giving me the biggest hug possible. I felt His love and warmth. It is one of the sweetest moments in my life.

Immediately after the meeting, I went to the bathroom mirror and started to learn how to smile. I never really smiled before, because I had no joy, no reason to smile. I remember my mind received a message: laughter is the closest thing to God's grace in the world. The Lord was already at work, changing me and guiding me to do the right thing—even to forgive my adoptive mother, and to love the people I did not love, including the Christians I had never liked. I understood love is an act of endless forgiveness.

It took me many years to really forgive my adoptive mother. When I thought about how my adoptive mother stole my childhood, I felt hurt. I did not want to hurt her. I tried to treat her kindly, but it was hard to say I loved her. I have prayed much about this because when you cannot forgive someone, you actually hurt more. Because I prayed sincerely, the Holy Spirit changed my heart. The Holy Spirit is the autocorrect mechanism. I began to look at things from my adoptive mother's perspective and just take it easy.

After two years of continuous prayer, God didn't point a gun at me, forcing me to forgive her. Instead, the Holy Spirit changed me. My adoptive mother did not trust me. She thought I would not care for her financially in her final years, but I did my best to serve her and treat her well until she went to be with our Lord in 1999.

Forgiveness is a spiritual lesson that is very hard to learn. Sometimes I would not forgive people because I hated them, or because I thought they did wrong. I later learned that in Chinese culture, including Hong Kong, hate is commonly integrated into the education system. China encourages hate education for its citizens, and it is one of the ideologies of CCP. Hate creates soul damage, from which it is very hard to recover. I am glad my Lord healed me. Abundant grace has accompanied me all the way.

6

BEGINNING TO SERVE

FUJIAN, CHINA, 2000

After a 1.5-hour bus ride, we arrived back in Fuqing. The police on the bus hadn't asked us any questions. We finally heard from Sun and the pastor who had my backpack. We knew they had fled when they were almost arrested by the police. They had hidden and looked for a safe way back to Fuqing. They reached out to house church Christians in the area and found a brother who was a government driver. He had a government car and could safely drive them back to Fuqing. We decided to meet at the house church where we had trained in Fuqing a couple of days earlier. Then we would drive the two hours back to Fuzhou together in the government car, and I would return to Hong Kong.

Thankful for our escape, we all met and prayed together. We ate and then quickly gathered our things to take the government car to Fuzhou. By the time we left, it was dark and there weren't many cars on the road. It was easy to see if we were being followed, although the chances of being followed were low, since we were in a government car. However, one car did seem to follow us. It was easy to spot because it had only one headlight. It continued to follow us, going wherever we did. Fortunately, we eventually lost the car.

At 9:30 p.m., we arrived at the small host home in Fuzhou, where Sun and I had stayed the first night. I entered the house, where the pastors had gathered to hear me teach. I asked if I could shower first, and if the sister could give me my Home Return Permit and plane ticket. The bathroom was on the first floor, while my permit and ticket were upstairs. So I took my shoes off to enter the bathroom downstairs, and the sister went upstairs to retrieve my permit and ticket.

This is when the front door burst open, as someone yelled for me to run. I ran as fast as I could out the back door, into the darkness, with the police close behind me. I didn't know how many others made it out, or where they were if they had.

My adrenaline surged, and I ran as fast as I could. I needed to stop and catch my breath. Seeing some empty homes, I quickly ducked behind one of them to hide. I tried to catch my breath as quietly as possible, my eyes and ears straining to see or hear the police who were chasing me. I could hear them! About three or four policemen had stopped running, and did not sound far. I had to be completely silent.

In the darkness, I prayed. I prayed God would give me the courage to persevere in faith and never betray my conscience. I asked God for forgiveness, because I felt responsible for this police raid happening. I prayed for the safety of the Christians in the house, and hoped they had escaped. I also prayed the police would not seize my Home Return Permit! I realized it was in the house in my backpack. I had no permit, no plane ticket, no way back to Hong Kong. The police were very likely to find it, learn my identity, and arrest me.

I heard the policemen turn and walk back in the direction of the house we had run from. In the silence, I asked myself what I was going to do. I didn't know this city or area at all, but I needed to move because the police might mount a search.

Then I heard a low voice close to me. It was Sun! Praise God! I had company.

Hong Kong, 1970s

The same night I accepted Christ, God called me to be a full-time pastor, as well as to serve the House Church in China. I was fifteen years old at the time, and I didn't really know what a "house church" was or what it meant to serve them. But God clearly put that calling into my heart and mind that night. I don't know how God did that, but I know He is almighty. It was as though He injected the name "house church" into my mind and heart so I could never forget it. From that day forward, the Holy Spirit reminded me daily of my life calling and ministry, which God had assigned for me.

At that time, it was expected for those who wanted to serve the Lord full time to go to Bible school. However, I was only fifteen and felt I was too young. If I graduated Bible school at nineteen, it would be difficult for me to pastor older men and women in the church. In Asian culture, youth and subordinates must always show deference and loyalty to their elders and superiors. This foundation of Asian society is deeply rooted in Confucianism and is prevalent in the church. This makes it difficult for young pastors to lead a church comprised of older members. Because of this, I decided to wait a few more years before I would attend seminary. In the meantime, I would serve in my home church in the Tai Po fishing village.

I began to visit churches in my area. I wanted to learn all I could from them, so I could help my church grow. Every Saturday, I went to our youth fellowship, and on Sunday, I would go to a different church. I knew that most of the so-called Christians in my church were not real Christians. They were not born again. They only wanted to take the relief goods given to the church by the Salvation Army. Others wanted to add God to the other gods they worshipped. They were superstitious and wanted the good luck that this other God named Jesus might bring them. They wanted help from Him when they were sick or needed money, but they didn't know Him as the One True God and Savior. They didn't understand His grace and mercy.

While I was visiting other churches, I met a man named John Bechtel. He was a missionary at the Christian and Missionary Alliance church in Tai Po at that time. John always made a great impression on people because he was a great speaker, spoke Cantonese very well (because he was born in Hong Kong), is a captivating storyteller, and has a charismatic personality. I was drawn to John and wanted to get to know him more. He invited me to visit a Christian camp he had just established in the New Territories, in order to minister to Hong Kong youth. He needed volunteers to care for the facilities and run the camp.

I visited the camp and began to work regularly as a volunteer. I was working at a boat factory at the time, which was actually illegal due to my age. A year later, in September of 1972, I was hired as the second full-time staff member of the camp.

Working at the Christian camp was hard. I started as the janitor—cleaning toilets, sweeping the floors, and maintaining the facilities. I painted the dormitories, the chapel, and the offices inside and out. Later, I did construction work at the camp. I built a miniature golf course, a rope bridge, and a rope course. I also planted trees and flowers as a gardener. I like gardening, and my wife, Margaret, does also. The first job in this world that God gave to Adam was gardening—caring for the Garden of Eden. Anything you can name at this camp, it has my work behind it. Later, I served as a counselor, Bible study leader, preacher, activity leader, administrator, and personnel manager. I worked at the camp from morning until night while also fulfilling my other responsibilities to my adoptive mother and to my church.

God used this time to build my character and teach me how to work with a team, resolve conflicts, build relationships, solve difficult problems, lead through crises, share the gospel, and head an organization.

When I first started working at the Christian camp, I was a young man who wanted to prove to everyone that I could do any job and do it well. I wanted their recognition and praise. I had an identity problem. I didn't know who I was, but I needed to prove myself to others. This created conflicts with my boss, coworkers, and friends because I didn't think they understood me. They didn't praise me when I did an excellent job. They didn't think as I did and that depressed me.

When I was sixteen years old, my best friend was Paul. We used to hike three times a week after work for three to four hours until after dark. One day, while we were hiking in the mountains, he asked me, "What is your definition of a friend?" I said, "A friend is someone who's willing to help you when you're in need."

Paul wasn't happy with my answer. He told me it sounded like I was using his friendship to serve myself, instead of seeing friendship as an opportunity to serve others. As we talked about it more, I realized he was right. At that time, I only saw a friend as someone who was willing to help me. I needed some help, but I never stopped to ask how I could help my friend. I was selfish and needed to repent.

When I was in elementary, middle, and high school, I didn't have many friends. I worked before and after school, and then went home as soon as I could. If I was late returning home, my mom would punish me for making less money. Because I gave her all my money, I didn't have money to go out to lunch with my classmates or even buy food to pack a lunch. My self-esteem was very low, so I separated myself from my classmates. I didn't want them to know my life, or ask me any questions I would have to answer.

But God was working in me. I observed and learned from the people around me. People came from all walks of life to this camp, including many pastors from different Christian denominations. Some of them were prideful and difficult to serve, because they never showed their appreciation. Others were so busy talking that they never listened. They only wanted to teach me how to do things they had never done themselves. Some would look down on the staff and me because we hadn't been to seminary. In their minds, we were only qualified to clean toilets. I still can't believe pastors would say such hurtful things, but it happened. Meanwhile, God was teaching me not to care what anyone said or thought of me. Instead, He wanted me to care about serving Him first, and also serving my boss, coworkers, and campers. God was training me for the work I would do in China, and my future interactions with different Chinese people, as well as people from all over the world. I praise Him for those years of teaching.

We all serve someone. Even when we serve God, we also serve earthly bosses, whom God has placed over us for His good reasons. These bosses helped to shape me into the man I am today, and I looked to them as spiritual advisors and mentors. However, they are human beings, just like me, and they had flaws, just like me. I tried to learn from them when I saw the good they did, but also I learned when I saw them make mistakes. My goal was not to find fault in others. We're all human—we do some things right and also make mistakes. But God brings people into our lives for different reasons. One of those reasons is for them to be an example to us.

One of my first bosses at the camp was very humorous and approachable. He took time to get to know others and have fun with them. He was also a great storyteller. However, like so many great storytellers, the line between fact and fiction, for entertainment purposes, was often blurred. He frequently exaggerated his real-life stories, and this troubled me. I was a quiet young man, shaped by my Confucian society, where social roles were clearly defined and hierarchies were strictly enforced. A younger person or junior employee could never challenge an older person or his boss. One day, I was in his office with other colleagues and boldly, but sincerely, asked him, "If a pastor exaggerates a story during one of his sermons and stretches the truth, does that count as lying?" His response was brief but given with a smile. He had no anger and let it pass.

This gave me a very good and deep impression of him, as I knew I had directly challenged his authority. I also knew that most other Chinese pastors would not have handled my confrontation well. But he did not scold, reprehend, or make me pay in any way. I had never experienced a superior that willfully behaved in this manner, and it made a lasting impression on me.

He was a hands-on boss in a place where there was much that needed to be done. We worked right alongside him as he did the work that the rest of us would do, such as cut grass and trim leaves. This was tiresome and laborious work that many pastors or missionaries (local and foreign) would never do, based on my observations growing up in a church.

My second boss gave me great latitude and freedom to develop and exercise my gifts. He respected my attitude of constant improvement and desire to do better at something each time. As a result, our work exceeded his expectations and requirements. Later, he also trusted me to handle all his personal finances when he went to study in the United States in 1977. He trusted my character, as well as my ability to get things done right.

He also understood that, while I was usually quiet, I would speak up on matters involving work efficiency, character, and godliness. He gave me ample opportunities to articulate my thoughts. He also had an open-door policy—I could speak with him anytime I asked. After I shared my thoughts on matters, he would make sensible adjustments to his directives for my colleagues and me.

He allowed me to run the camp as the director while he was studying in the United States, even though he was the director. This was not because he was lazy or disregarded his responsibilities. He had to attend meetings with other Christian leaders around Hong Kong and abroad, and his work at the camp consisted primarily of preaching and holding meetings with senior staff. I was responsible for the other administrative and gospel camp matters.

Eventually, we had about six full-time staff members working at the Christian camp. We received many phone calls from people who wanted information about the camp, prices, and activities, and needed to make bookings. But I was young and very quiet. I didn't like talking and didn't want to talk to people on the phone.

I finally asked my boss if it was possible for me not to talk on the phone, because I hated it so much. He listened to me, and from that day on, I didn't have to take phone calls. At the time, it was a relief to me, but eventually I regretted my decision. I had limited myself. I hadn't seen it as an opportunity to force myself to grow more comfortable and confident when speaking to people. I didn't view public speaking as an asset God could use in my life. I only thought of how much I hated it.

It was a hard lesson for me to learn. We all have likes and dislikes. We all have things we don't want to do—the very thought of which makes us nervous or not want to get out of bed in the morning. But if we do them, we get better at them and grow more confident. We may even find we like them and see God using them for His glory. We should never limit ourselves. When we limit ourselves, we are limiting the ways God can use us. I have learned not to limit myself by only doing what I like. Our Lord has unlimited resources, and I believe He has many plans. He is looking for loyal servants who can carry out His plans. I am already preparing myself physically, mentally, and spiritually so I can go to war with Satan anytime God calls me to fight the battle alongside Him.

Later, I worked as the camp chef for about two years. I had

previously cooked for my mom, godsister, and her family, but I had always hated cooking. At the camp, I had to cook for 200 campers every day, including planning the menu, buying food, and even cleaning the dishes. I woke up at 5 a.m. to cook congee (Chinese rice porridge) for breakfast for the campers two to three days a week. Besides cooking, I had my other work, planning, and staff management duties.

Why didn't I like to cook? It wasn't the workload or low pay. It was because I knew people looked down on me because I was a cook. If I were speaking at the chapel or attending Christian conferences in a nice suit, I would appear successful. Because of this inner struggle, I didn't like to cook.

Yet my Lord trained me to know it didn't matter how others looked at me. The important thing was my loyalty and faithful service to Him. I learned that to serve others humbly is to release your right to yourself. I was willing to submit myself to my Lord and obey His orders even though I didn't like to cook. I cooked for Him and for the campers.

Luis Palau and Billy Graham were two great evangelists that the Lord has used to proclaim the gospel all over the world. Both came to Hong Kong while I was working at the camp. I had the honor to work for both of their events, which brought together almost every evangelical church of Hong Kong as well as many non-believers who accepted Christ.

I served as assistant field director for the first crusade, which meant I was working behind the scenes. I secured the donation box, arranged chairs on the platform, prepared follow-up forms, printed and hung banners, and did everything else you could think of. This kind of work didn't attract many volunteers, but our staff members were willing to do it. I really enjoyed working with my colleagues at these two big six-day events.

The willingness to serve was the attitude that defined our team. We didn't care who took the credit. Many even took our service for granted, but we didn't care. We knew we were doing it for our Lord. Non-believers becoming Christians was our reward, and it was worth the long hours to see the joy of people coming to know our Lord. It made us forget how tired we were.

If we look around and see that work is not being done, our first thought shouldn't be, "That work isn't my responsibility." No, we need to do it ourselves. Don't worry about how others might look at you when you're sweaty, dirty, and stinky instead of being the one on the platform, in the choir, or on TV. You may not want others to take your photo while you are moving chairs, putting on tablecloths, or hanging up the banners, but all the work is important. Each person is part of the puzzle, which would be incomplete if each piece did not work together.

Learning to be humble and to serve wherever God asks me is the key to serving the house churches in China. Going into the villages to preach, with no modern toilet or shower for days, and restless nights on a hard bed with no mattress or good pillow is part of the work too. How can I complain when Jesus didn't have a pillow either?

I worked at the camp for the next twenty-three years. They were some of the best years of my life. From 1990 to 1995, I was invited to speak at many Christian camps in Japan, South Korea, Taiwan, Australia, and the United States about Christian camping in Hong Kong. I shared how we used the camp year-round to bring Christ to people from all walks of life.

This Christian camp is where God taught me how to be a servant. In ministry, we try to be humble and use the term "servant leadership." I have read at least ten books about servant leadership and management, but how do we even define servant leadership?

Management and leadership are hot topics. Many people want to know how to manage people . . . because they want to be the leader, which includes myself. I wanted to know how to be a good manager and an effective leader. In graduate school, I read many Harvard business school case studies, and I learned management and leadership strategies from a business perspective.

But the world is changing. Each generation looks at leadership from a very different perspective, which makes my learning continuous. It seems there is no end to this subject. In my understanding, management and leadership are not the same thing — they are very different. Management is about planning, while leadership is about inspiring. Managers have people who work for them, while leaders have people who follow them. It's easy for me to be a good manager, but it is not easy to be a good leader and to keep your vision and goals alive in your followers. Leadership is also the ability of a manager to induce the team to work with confidence and zeal. A leader has followers, can motivate people and show them what to do, can implement good ideas, and can make good moves and changes.

In politics, leadership is equal to the use of power. No matter how they obtain their leadership positions, politicians exercise their power. But from my point of view, they are not leaders if they do not have a vision and cannot motivate people to follow them. They are just managers. Leaders are hard to find, and few people are qualified.

Communist China believes the leaders who rule China are elites, and that their decisions are best for China. No one could be better than them. But they are probably not the elites of China. Even if they are, without moral standards, highly educated people just commit sin more wisely. In the last fifteen to twenty years, millions of Chinese have obtained their master's degrees and PhDs in the West. They know how to be corrupt without being caught. They make decisions selfishly and for their own good. If a nation cannot accept its people speaking the truth, it will soon turn into a tragedy.

The basic contradiction between fundamentalism and

universal values is that fundamentalism does not allow betrayal. There is no room for discussion or disagreement. The leader's opinion, ideology, and decision are unarguable.

Because I've served as a pastor, as well as in management positions at the camp and at a non-governmental organization (NGO), people have considered me a leader. Of course, I am not a political leader of a big country with millions of people, or the CEO of a big company with thousands of employees. I am just a small potato and a servant of my Lord.

While working at the Christian camp, I also served the communities of the New Territories by participating in anti-corruption, anti-crime, and anti-drug campaigns. I also helped run programs and fun days for people to come to the park to learn how to be good citizens of Hong Kong. I also worked with the government to run Chinese New Year's fun and game days for the community.

Because of my many years of serving Hong Kong, my service was recognized and honored by the community, and I was elected as Outstanding Young Man of the North District in 1985. I was also appointed by the Hong Kong government to serve on the North District board as district counselor for two years, on the committee for the social welfare division.

I served with all my heart and brought changes to the committee. Because they all knew I was a Christian, I had good opportunities to share the gospel and represent God. But after two years, I quit because there were many political fights over power with which I didn't want to be involved. I was young at the time, but two congressmen wanted me to be their assistant and each offered me a large salary. However, I knew my calling was to serve the Lord in ministry. I couldn't do that as a politician. I didn't need to pray about their offer. I already knew I wasn't the right person. It was a slight temptation, but in the end, it was easy to say no and follow God.

7

TEN SENTENCES A WEEK

WISCONSIN, USA, 1980

In 1980, I had the opportunity to travel to the United States, to audit outdoor activities and camp counselor classes through Wheaton College in Illinois. I attended a two-day orientation at Wheaton, and then traveled by myself to Wisconsin for the outdoor training. I had never been to the United States before, and at that time, it was a big deal for someone from Asia like me to travel there. On that same trip, I visited Camp-of-the-Woods, a North American organization that financially supported our camp. I had heard of Camp-of-the-Woods during my nine years working at camp. They sponsored my trip to the United States, and it was great to visit their facility and learn from them. I later developed a golf course at our camp based on theirs. While visiting Camp-of-the-Woods, I felt the love from my Christian family overseas. It was a spiritually high moment for me.

This was an amazing trip for me because I had always loved sports, especially soccer and basketball. Working at the Christian camp in Hong Kong gave me amazing opportunities to work with many North American athletes and coaches, whose basketball and baseball teams traveled to China for friendly matches with their Chinese counterparts. From 1988–1993, I served as the assistant coach and translator for the Guangdong women's basketball team, and from 1988–1994, I worked with the Guangzhou baseball team. I was invited to China to visit the Chinese athletic facilities and work with the national sports teams. I would invite players and coaches to the Three-Self churches on Sundays, and would get to know the pastors of the Three-Self churches as well. This was my stepping-stone into China when it was just beginning to open up, but my work was still very secretive.

Through these volunteer sporting activities, God gave me a wider first-hand view of the world, especially of North American and Chinese culture. I saw the vast difference between the cultures. At the time, all Chinese athletes were recruited by the Chinese government, but in draconian and arbitrary ways. For instance, if you were tall and even somewhat athletic, you would be recruited to play basketball. By "recruited," I mean, "forced to play basketball." You may not like basketball, know anything about basketball, or even want to play basketball, but that didn't matter. Your desires meant nothing. Show up and do as you are told. The families actually didn't mind this arrangement, because it meant the government took care of their children and relieved their financial burden. However, the recruit was forced to endure arduous routines beginning at 5am, verbal abuse, and unscientific and ineffective coaching methods mandated by high-ranking officials with no sports knowledge. Recruits faced intense pressure to succeed, in order to save face and not shame their country. If they failed, there were consequences.

The Chinese coaches and officials loved to compete, but they wanted to win—and to win big. In reality, "friendly" games between the Chinese and North American teams were not friendly at all. These games were usually basketball, baseball, and tennis. Even if the visiting North American team was a high school team, the Chinese officials would pit them against a Chinese national adult team in order to win at all costs. Speaking of costs, the officials would then tally up large expenses and claim them for "hospitality" reasons.

My involvement in sports ministry also led me to volunteer at the Castle Peak Boy's Home in Hong Kong every Tuesday night for two years in 1988 and 1989. After attending a coaching camp in Fresno, California, I was invited by the supervisor of the boys' home to come work with the boys.

These boys had committed crimes, and were serving sentences

ranging from six months to two years. Even though it was a government detention center, the supervisor allowed us to evangelize the boys directly with no red tape. So I, along with my friends and coworkers Harry and Jumbo, went to the home of about fifty boys and invited them to play basketball. About half of them would show up, and it was chaotic. They didn't follow any of the rules, they fought with each other, and some tried to strip naked to play basketball. They ran wild most of the time, so it was difficult to minister to them.

Due to privacy laws, we couldn't ask the boys what crimes they had committed. We couldn't leave our contact information for the boys, or ask them for their contact information. We also couldn't have Bible studies with them, but they were far too restless for that anyways. Instead, we would treat them to soft drinks after we played basketball, which made them happy because soft drinks were a rare treat. That gave us five to ten minutes to share the gospel with the boys. Some of them did make a verbal confession to accept Christ, and some showed up consistently over extended periods of time, really improving their basketball skills and behavior. Even though my ministry time there was short and I had limited time to share the gospel, all three of us felt it was worthwhile work, because those boys had few opportunities and few people cared about them.

Back in 1980, when I visited the United States for the first time, the camp counselor training was held near Lake Superior in Wisconsin. It lasted for six weeks, three of which were spent in the classroom, and three of which were spent outside hiking and rock climbing. On Fridays, each student had to go out alone and survive in the woods. It was an eye-opening trip for me as a young man to travel solo internationally, and it was a good opportunity for me to practice my English.

I loved the athletics of hiking and rock climbing, but that didn't mean it was easy. We were high up in the mountains and had to scale a 200-foot cliff (with a safety rope). I was scared to go up. I wanted to go down, back to safety. But an interesting fact about rock climbing is that it's often much safer to keep climbing up than to retreat down. On the first day of rock climbing, it took me six tries to overcome my fears and climb to the top, but my classmates encouraged me the whole time. Without a team behind me, I never would have done it.

However, I went from those times of team encouragement during the week to total isolation on the weekends. The teacher would go with us the first day to teach different survival methods, but then we had to split up and be on our own. He would check on each student the second day, just long enough to make sure we were okay.

I grew up feeling alone. Being by myself was nothing new, but I was in a radically different environment from Hong Kong. Instead of being alone and surrounded by people, buildings, and the noise of the city, I was alone and surrounded by dense woods, silence, and thoughts of bears and other animals. I was overwhelmed by the beauty around me. I loved the sunrises and sunsets. I had time for wonderful reflection on God and prayer. With nothing else to distract me, I grew very close to God.

I spent six weeks pushing through my fear, focusing on my next firm grip on the rocks, and not thinking of what would happen if I fell. The fear and isolation taught me to focus on God and persevere, no matter what the circumstances were. God used these six weeks to prepare me in ways I would only comprehend much later.

FUJIAN, CHINA, 2000

Sun and I waited in the darkness by the abandoned houses. We talked about our options. We were still close to the host family house, but we were sure the police were still there. I needed my Home Return Permit, but there was little chance I could retrieve it, let alone everything else in my backpack. We also couldn't stay where we were. The police would return, knowing some had fled on foot, and were probably not far away. We decided our best option was to travel by foot to the next village as fast as we could.

We walked and ran for the next thirty minutes. When we felt a little safer with the distance, we stopped to rest and reevaluated our situation. I told Sun that I couldn't leave China without my Home Return Permit. In 2000, I was living in the United States, but I had stayed with friends in Hong Kong before traveling into China. I had left my Hong Kong passport and return ticket to the U.S. with my friends back in Hong Kong. I hadn't wanted to bring them into China for fear of losing them, or of the Chinese police finding out more about me. I had no option but to return to Hong Kong. There was only one province between Fujian and Hong Kong, Guangdong. I decided my best option was to try to go to Guangzhou, a city in Guangdong about two hours away from the Hong Kong border. I could call my friends at the Christian camp, and perhaps one or two of them could cross the border, meet me in Guangzhou, and help me get back into Hong Kong. Sun offered to travel with me.

It was still late at night, and there was no transportation available. We walked through muddy and rocky fields. I was still barefoot; my feet were wet, cold, and dirty. While Sun was a mainland Chinese and didn't need to fear drawing attention to himself, I couldn't take any chances, so I had to lie face-down whenever we saw bicycle headlights or people approaching on foot. If they saw I was a foreigner, they would call the police. I had to lie down immediately wherever I was, regardless of whether the ground was muddy, wet, or rocky. Twice in my haste I even landed face-first in cow manure!

Sun called two of the sisters that had accompanied us earlier in the week, and they said they had a Christian friend—a taxi driver—who lived in a village about a three-hour walk away. If we could get there on foot, he could help us. We couldn't go back. We had to trust God. We had to press on.

It was 1 a.m. when we finally reached the home of the Christian taxi driver. We were exhausted, dirty, and unsure of what to do next, but we prayed together for one hour. We prayed for the other believers who had also been at the host house, as well as for a miracle that my Home Return Permit would somehow be released and returned to me. We then discussed how to leave the city, but were too tired and fell asleep. We slept for two hours until the ringing of a telephone woke us up.

HONG KONG, 1970s

Believe it or not, from the time I was five to fifteen, I probably only spoke about ten sentences a week. I didn't enjoy speaking because when I spoke to my adoptive mother, I was wrong no matter what and would be punished for it. I learned from a very young age that it was better to be quiet.

But when I became a Christian, I was on fire for the gospel. It was a fire from the Lord, and it pushed me to work hard for Him. I had already worked hard since I was a little boy, and I was used to it. Now I felt God was pushing me to work hard for His kingdom and was granting me the wisdom, power, and passion to proclaim the gospel. To share the gospel meant I needed to talk to people, including complete strangers. I didn't want to do it, but I knew I could not just attend church as if I were watching a sports game on TV—eating snacks and drinks, but not running the game myself and getting sweaty and tired. I knew I had to change myself by the power of the Holy Spirit.

Otherwise, I could be going to church but not know Jesus.

I really wanted to do any kind of work for the Lord other than speaking, but there was a strong pull within me to preach the gospel and share the good news. I was fearful, but it was my job and assignment. It was difficult for me to change that part of me. I had to learn to be talkative, and I didn't like it. It went against my nature, and I didn't know how to overcome it. Just like I didn't want to talk on the phones at the camp in Hong Kong, I didn't want to talk to others, but I did want to evangelize. I knew I had to push on, and to trust God to overcome my fear.

I learned that John Bechtel was conducting a seminar to teach Christians how to share the gospel by using the Four Spiritual Laws. I immediately applied for the seminar and was accepted. It was a three-day seminar, and on the last day, I made a commitment to God. I committed to speak with ten random people on the street within the next week.

That was a difficult commitment to keep. At times, I regretted it and wanted to forget it. But through God's strength, I followed through for seven days and talked to ten people, mostly on the bus, and mostly men—I didn't want to talk to women because I thought they were all mean like my mom. My approach was simple. I read from the Four Spiritual Laws booklet and asked them if they wanted Jesus to be their Savior. Seven of them said yes, and four of these men still attend church in Hong Kong to this day.

I realized I was useless on my own. I didn't want to speak to anyone about anything, let alone to strangers about Jesus. But when I gave my life and my soul to Jesus Christ, He made me useful. God can use each person greatly for His kingdom, but never by a person's own power. It will always be through God's power, and in situations where we have to depend completely on Him. My lips were trembling as I read from the little booklet on the bus, but the result was eternal. It was, and everything we accomplish is, by the grace of God and the power of the

Holy Spirit. It is not about me, but about God receiving all the glory, when I submit to Him and am used by Him accordingly. This is an important spiritual lesson that my Lord taught me. It affects my whole life.

Along with evangelism, God gave me a desire to preach and teach, which meant I had to talk even more and in front of people. I didn't have any theological training then. I had read the Bible since I was a boy, but not as a Christian. But I began to read the Bible with a love for God, His Word, and His church in my heart. I found commentaries to understand more. I prayed and asked God to equip me to teach the people at my church to understand the gospel so they could have a personal relationship with Christ — so they could really be Christians and know the love of God. This made the deacons of my church happy. As I said before, they were lazy and hypocritical. They had relied on guest pastors, many of whom were wolves in sheep's clothing, and allowed them into the church. But in me, they had a volunteer who was on fire to teach and preach. They didn't care that I had no formal theological training. They only cared about someone else doing the work. They made me preach two Sundays each month, teach Sunday school, and lead the Saturday night youth fellowship.

There were about ten teenagers in the youth fellowship, and we had known each other for about three years. I made sure they understood salvation and the Bible. Because I wanted the fellowship and church to grow, we went out to the non-believers in the village, which for us were people on boats, and invited them to our fellowship and evangelized. We made the fellowship fun and creative with interesting debates and discussions, interactive games, and always a Bible study and sermon.

We gave our best to God and the fellowship, and many new people attended and became Christians. More came every Saturday to learn more about God. What began as a group of ten quickly grew to sixty people. People from other towns began to attend. Eventually, Christians came from other churches to learn how to grow their church, but we had no secret. We had no master plan. We told them, "We just do our best and let God do the rest." I was a youth with no theological training, and lips that trembled when I had to speak to others. But I had God and His Holy Spirit working through me, to overcome my fear and use me however He saw fit.

8

HOW COULD I FORGIVE HER?

Fujian, China, 2000

Back at the taxi driver's house, it was almost 4 a.m. when the phone rang. Someone who had been in the neighborhood called and confirmed that two women from the host house had been arrested and were in the police station. The police had searched the whole house and seized my computer, backpack, and many other things. Not only the police, but also city officials, soldiers, and many government cars still surrounded the house. We were exhausted and upset, but we praised the Lord that most who fled were safe, at least for the moment.

The taxi driver gave me a pair of shoes to wear. They were too small for me, but I was thankful. We started out for Guangzhou city in Guangdong Province. Two house church sisters, who were neighbors of the taxi driver, volunteered to accompany us as far as Xiamen, and then Sun and I would continue on to Guangzhou.

There were few cars on the road in the early morning. The driver was alert and kept his eye on the rearview mirror. He suddenly looked into the mirror suspiciously and said we were being followed. We turned around to look, and sure enough, two cars were following us. Whenever we turned, they turned; wherever we stopped, they stopped. After twenty minutes, we were very sure we were being followed. I then asked our driver to drive faster and take a quick turn off onto any small road, and Sun and I would jump out of the car and run. The two house church sisters, who were

Chinese citizens and lived in Fujian, would not be in any danger. They agreed to continue in the car as if nothing had happened.

The driver found a small road and quickly turned. Sun and I jumped out of the car. We ran to a small farmhouse, where we hid until we were sure the cars were not returning to look for us. We didn't have a map and weren't sure where to go. We had to find the main highway so we could take a bus to Xiamen. We started walking.

We walked for about thirty minutes and reached a main road. We got on a bus and it took us to Quanzhou, a large city north of Xiamen. Here we charged our mobile phones, bought telephone cards and spare batteries, and ate some bread we bought. We rested in a shop for about half an hour and then started walking to the bus station that would take us to Xiamen.

As we walked, we noticed someone following us on foot. But he followed at a distance and didn't try to stop us and ask us questions. When we had a chance, we ran and hid until we lost him. We didn't want to risk taking a bus to Xiamen, since the secret police probably knew that's where we were headed.

With the help of local house church Christians, we took bicycles, motorcycles, and small farm trucks, changing our routes and vehicles often. When we finally felt safe, we decided to take a taxi the rest of the way to Xiamen. Because Xiamen was a large city on the southern border of Fujian and Guangdong provinces, once we were there, we could take public transportation like a bus or train to Guangzhou.

On the three-hour drive, I had time to sleep, pray, and reflect.

I had been chased by the secret police for about a day, but it already seemed much longer. Yet the Christians, for whom I came to China to serve and teach, lived under this threat day and night as they served God and the church. But they were not bitter or angry at the constant harassment of the Chinese government. They didn't pray down God's wrath or destruction on the officials that arrested and separated them from their families and church. They forgave them, and prayed that their oppressors would come to know Jesus as their Lord.

This is one striking feature of persecuted Christians in China — they never pray for persecution to end. They pray for God to give them strength, uphold their testimony, and for forgiveness for their persecutors.

Hong Kong, 1970–80s

The furthest I've ever been from home is nothing compared to the distance between my adoptive mother and me. Between the ages of five to fifteen, I had no male influence in my life except for the guest pastors and deacons at my church. Even from a young age, I knew they were bad men. I wasn't sure exactly why those men were bad at the time. Maybe it was God's wisdom that told me, "These are not good examples for you. Never do what they do!"

My adoptive mother had psychological issues. She had no children of her own, and in those days, it was a serious problem if a woman could not give birth. She suffered from the social stigma associated with childlessness. The village and church gossip about her made her overly emotional and unstable.

She looked angry every day and naturally had a very bad temper, but because she was a pastor's wife, she would pretend to be nice in front of the congregation. I learned the word *hypocrite* when I was very young, and believed she was a hypocrite. She had two faces — the nice face in front of people and the angry face in private, which reflected her anger at God and others around her. She complained every day that others had better lives than she did and that people treated her badly. Everyone else was at fault, including me.

She abused me every day—verbally, emotionally, and physically. I served as her stress and anger release. I counted it a fortunate day if she didn't abuse me. After ten years, I think I only experienced a few of those days. Even when I was fifteen years old and attending high school, she would still beat me at night for no reason. When I started to work at the Christian camp, I stayed at the camp so I wouldn't have to face her and her anger. But she asked me to come back home every week to have dinner or lunch with her, and to give 90 percent of my salary to her. I didn't want to come home, but I had to. She would always tell me, "Although I'm not your real mother, I'm your mother who raised you, and you need to remember me and thank me!" I knew I had worked so hard myself to earn a living for us since I was six, but I never argued with her.

Later, my wife Margaret would ask me, "Why didn't you just run away from home? You were earning money for yourself. You could have survived!" But I had to be careful because I was pastoring the church, and didn't want people to think I was mistreating my mother or disrespecting her. It was impossible to tell others the truth, because they would never believe she was unloving and abusive. From the way she treated me publically, no one knew the trouble I faced or my sorrow. But Jesus did. Later, my youth fellowship members learned the truth as they observed her and knew what I said was true. However, because she was a pastor's wife, no one wanted to confront her because she was a "servant of God."

For many years, my adoptive mother didn't want me to know who my real parents were and would tell me different stories. She was insecure and thought I would leave her and not care for her. I was her social security, and she didn't want to give that up. My real family was also careful about my situation, and my parents never asked me to visit them or said they wanted a reunion.

When I was thirteen, I received a letter from my younger biological sister in the mail. The letter was sent to me at the church, and fortunately, I was the one who picked up the mail every day. Had my adoptive mother seen the letter first, I might not have ever received it. When I had previously received letters from my biological family and my adoptive mother found out, she had become angry and hit me.

My sister wrote that she and my entire real family wanted to meet me. I didn't know how to deal with it or what to do next. But I started thinking about meeting them. I finally knew for sure the *So* family was my real family. I was excited, but also worried, because I didn't know what it would be like to meet them officially for the first time.

I wanted to connect with them, but I didn't know how to start the conversation. I felt like an island. I didn't want to show my feelings to anyone. I had already had a hard life full of suffering, and because of that, I felt nothing could make me happy or give me excitement. I wasn't used to sharing, and instead kept my thoughts and feelings inside of me.

I went to my biological family's village when I was fifteen. By now, they lived in housing the government had built for the local fishermen and their families. They were excited to see me and warmly welcomed me into their home and lives. We ate together, and they were very talkative with me. I was still unsure how to deal with it, but I began to visit them regularly after that and slowly built relationships with them.

My two older biological sisters always tried to talk to me and care for me. I wanted a hug from them, but I was too shy to ask. I also wanted a hug from my biological mother, but I never received one. My wife Margaret knows I need her hugs very much because I never had a mother who would hug me. I really missed the personal touch from my biological mother. Because I didn't grow up with my biological brothers and sisters, there was always some distance between us, but we loved each other and were very open to each other. We talked about everything and loved and respected each other.

By God's grace, I have never blamed my real parents or my grandfather for giving me away. I don't know why. I do know it's not because of the education. It is because of God's grace and His plan. But it was important for me to never hate my biological family. Believe it or not, I never had any negative feelings toward my biological parents. God gave me the wisdom to understand that hating them would be sinful and detrimental. It is often said, "Bitterness is a poison we drink ourselves, hoping someone else will die." I knew it was true, and God's grace kept me from that poison. I knew there had to be a good reason for them to give me away, like the fact I was sick and near death until God healed me.

Although I do not have any bitter feelings against my real family—I know they love and accept me—there is no way to recover the lost fifteen years of family relationships, especially when we were young.

My sisters and brothers did not have the opportunity to earn a high school education. However, all of them are very smart, and two of my brothers have succeeded in their work, becoming managers of two big manufacturing companies. My older brother was also awarded an honorary degree from Hong Kong Baptist University several years ago. We now meet regularly in Hong Kong whenever I am available. They all love me very much, and I am thankful for them. It has not been an easy journey, but I am glad God gave me back my real family.

I also had to forgive my adoptive mother. One way I learned to forgive her was by finding reasons to justify what she did to me, and trying to understand her anxiety and psychological issues. Sometimes it worked and sometimes it didn't. When I was away from her, I could forget about her, so it seemed to me I had forgiven her. I was a happy person when I was away from her. I filled my day with work, sports, and outdoor things like hiking. It helped me to be a healthy and happy person. God's grace was with me. He taught me many things, because I had no family in my life who could give me advice.

I did pray hard, because I didn't want to sin against God by not treating her properly, according to His standard. After I became a Christian, I learned how to truly forgive her. She really didn't know what she was doing. This was one of Jesus' statements when He was on the cross. When I began to forgive, to truly forgive her, then real joy flooded my heart.

Much later, when I was married with two sons, my wife Margaret and I asked my adoptive mother to stay with my family, and live just outside the camp in an apartment. It was a good decision, because by then she was more than ninety years old. We wanted her to feel loved and not forgotten. In Chinese culture, sons and daughters are every parent's social security. She was worrying too much, and we wanted her to feel happy and feel secure. She lived with us for five years, until our family left for the United States in 1995.

At that time, we put her in a senior home and paid for all the expenses. I never knew how much money she had because her goddaughter was in charge of her finances. She gave me 7,000 U.S. dollars and said she had saved this money for me. Other than that, I never received anything from her. I paid for everything she ever needed. But I have no regrets. God taught me to be generous, and to never count the accumulation of money as important in my life. I took care of her until she passed away in 1999 at ninety-eight years old. My whole family returned to Hong Kong for her funeral service. I had done everything I could as a son to treat her well.

I thank God for putting my adoptive mother in my life. I believe His purpose was to train me to love someone I did not like. It was a good experience and valuable training for me. When I look back, I have no regrets.

I'm actually glad that I went through that because it made

me a better man. As I grew spiritually, I learned that the greatest pain is not in suffering, but in unwillingness and disobedience. I learned to follow my Lord with a willing attitude, and accept His arrangement for my life so that it will be full of His peace. These experiences made me more like Jesus, and for that, I'm grateful.

I have learned that forgiveness means to give up your right to yourself. This has been one of the most difficult spiritual lessons for me to learn, but perhaps the most valuable.

9

MEETING MARGARET

FUJIAN, CHINA, 2000

While Sun and I were in the taxi headed to Xiamen, a pastor called to tell us that my Home Return Permit had somehow been given to a house church sister. I told him that once we got on a bus in Xiamen, we would be on our way to Guangzhou. I asked him to call again in the evening so we could set up a safe place to meet in Guangzhou.

It was a miracle the police never seized my permit, but I didn't learn the whole story until much later. Close to the bathroom on the first floor of the house, there was a small square white table. When the police entered, most of us were able to escape. However, the house owner had gone upstairs to retrieve my permit. She was arrested, along with her twelve-year-old daughter, who had been sleeping upstairs. In the commotion, the house owner had thrown my permit on the table. There it had lain, out in the open, while 150 police officers and officials went in, around, and out of the house. None of them had seen it.

Later, about 1:30 a.m., a teenage boy from next door (and a relative of the homeowner), being curious, walked over to the house to see what all the commotion had been about. He walked right past two police officers guarding the door and into the house. He saw the permit on the table, picked it up, and recognized my photo because we had seen each other earlier. When I heard about him later, I remembered him too, because he had been wearing a pair of Sony Walkman headphones, which were popular back then, and his hair was dyed. He slipped my permit into his pocket. He walked back out, and then called some of the pastors, telling them that he had my permit. This whole time, the police officers did not appear to see him.

We arrived at the train station in Xiamen, but found there was no direct train to Guangzhou. There was a bus, but it would take nineteen hours to travel to Guangzhou. Traveling on a bus in China for nineteen hours was a miserable proposition. It was an old bus with no air conditioning and no bathroom, which would drive along unfinished potholed roads. It would be crammed with people who brought chickens and other animals along, but it was the safest way. It was impossible to go by taxi, because the distance was more than 700 miles. Also, we could not trust a taxi driver. Many taxi drivers would rob their passengers on long journeys.

While we rode on the bus, I called two of my friends at the camp in Hong Kong, and asked if they could meet me in Guangzhou with some clean clothes and a larger pair of shoes. I asked them to stay in a hotel and wait for my arrival at around 5–6 a.m. on Friday morning. I also called the house church in Fuzhou, and asked if two people could fly to Guangzhou the next morning, instead of taking a bus for nineteen hours. It would save time, because I needed to leave China and return to Hong Kong as quickly as possible. They all agreed it was the best plan, and I happily paid for all their travel expenses. Finally, I called Margaret to tell her I was safe and almost home. Cramped and tired on the bus, breathing in the diesel fumes, I was ready to be home and see my wife and two boys again.

Hong Kong, 1970–80s

I didn't grow up with an understanding of what "family" was. I didn't really know what it meant to have a family until I had a family of my own. It was then that God helped me understand marriage and family, which are gifts from God. But He does not give us a pre-built family. Instead, He gives us the *materials* to build a family, and asks us to spend our lives building a family for His glory.

When I was young and working at the Christian camp, I lived in the dormitories. I had a great friend named Jack. Jack would always visit me after he finished work, and we would talk until three or four in the morning. We would talk about our future, and about what we wanted to do with our lives. I was on fire for the gospel and wanted to serve the camp and my church. When we talked about dating and marriage, I told Jack that I was too young to think about it, and the only women I had known in my life were abusive and mean. I thought all women were like that, and I wasn't sure I wanted to marry. If I did marry, I thought maybe I could when I was around thirty years old.

However, love is like running water—hard to stop once it starts. One day in the summer of 1976, I was at the camp when I met Margaret, a girl who had just been hired to work at the camp office. I fell in love the first time I saw her.

From that moment on, I made sure I took every opportunity to be at the camp. I was in love and wanted to spend every moment I could with her. When I couldn't go, I would call her and pretend to be someone interested in booking the camp just so I could hear her voice. After a while, she knew who it was and played along. I thought that was a better sign than her hanging up on me.

I soon asked her to go out on a date with me. She said yes, and my plan was to take her to Lamma Island, an island off the coast of Hong Kong with nice places for picnics. There were only two ferries for Lamma Island each day, one in the morning and one in the evening. So I knew I would have seven hours with Margaret on the island. It was a good opportunity for us to get to know each other, away from work and other distractions. I didn't want this opportunity to slip away from me. The sea was rough on the way out to Lamma Island, and the ferry rocked back and forth. I reached out and took Margaret's hand to help steady her, and she never let go. It was a good first date.

I was in love with Margaret and wanted to marry her, but my boss at the camp told me she wasn't suitable for me, and I should choose another girl. He went so far as to say she didn't "look" spiritual, and I needed a girl who looked like a pastor's wife. But I disagreed with him. I didn't think it was right to judge people by their appearance. My boss had always valued people who were good looking and well spoken, but he saw people like me as only menial workers.

I'm glad I listened to God and not my boss. Since I was five years old, I've had to make decisions on my own, and I knew better than to listen to bad advice. I made the decision, knowing that God had brought Margaret into my life to marry her.

While we dated, we had moments of difficulties, and almost broke up at times. However, I prayed and knew she was to be my wife. I started to change many of my bad habits in order for her to be sure I was the right man for her to marry. At the time, I thought I was already changing a lot. But it took time for me to change my character, the ways I communicated with her, and my bad habits.

It was a hot day on August 9, 1981 when we were married at the Christian camp. It was an outdoor wedding, and the stifling Hong Kong heat and humidity made Margaret's makeup run. The cameraman botched the film, resulting in only a handful of photos that our friends had taken. But I didn't care. We were married and so happy.

The cover of our wedding program (designed by Barnabas)

During those days in Hong Kong, marriage counseling wasn't popular. I didn't believe in counselors. I believed God was my Counselor, and trusted Jesus to guide us through our life and marriage together. I knew that love was never ending. My love for Margaret should never change, except to increase. I knew marriage was for a lifetime. I might change my house, my job, or my citizenship, but I would never change my wife. We signed a contract in front of God. It is a lifetime lesson of how to grow and maintain a relationship with the one you love the most. Marriage is a relationship that's very hard, and must be kept with care. However, I believe God has used marriage to mold my life and behavior. Only God can help me to overcome my evil side with good, because marriage also means a deeper relationship with Jesus. He is our matchmaker and maintainer.

I knew that no matter what, Margaret was to be the most important person in my life, and I always needed to handle our marriage with care. I only have a certain amount of time and energy per day, and I can only really please one person a day. That person needed to be Margaret. So the goal and success of my life was to make my better half smile and grow in joy every day.

Margaret is beautiful inside and out. Everyone can see her outer beauty, but only I know just how beautiful she is on the inside. She doesn't like speaking in front of large groups of people, but she can talk to me for hours. She does not spend much time with friends, because I'm not only her husband, but also her best friend. She supports me and is eager to follow God's calling together. She works hard behind the scenes to make me successful in my ministry and never wants credit. I try my best every day not to disappoint her.

I enjoy eating meals with Margaret. I like to date her every day. I enjoy cooking and eating breakfast with her every day — one egg over easy with one piece of toast, one homemade latte, and prayer.

Our good friend Jumbo, a Hong Kong board member of our HC Ministry*, always said, "When I came to the camp for the first time, I saw a village lady dressed up like a farmer, and she was gardening and pulling weeds in the flower bed. When I asked her where the office was, she pointed me in the right direction. Later on, the camp staff asked me, 'Do you know who the lady is working under the hot sun in the garden?' I told them I didn't know, and they told me, 'She's the director's wife!' I couldn't believe the director's wife was working in the hot Hong Kong sun and doing work the staff would normally do." This is Margaret. This is her character. This is how she works every day for the ministry.

Margaret supported my vision of using photography as a tool for the gospel when it was not common. With my 35mm Pentax camera and some A/V equipment, Margaret and I made our first gospel slide show at the camp. We wrote a script together and added pop music for the score. Then we used two projectors at the same time to tell the story.

We had the privilege of using this gospel slide show at the Christian camp every Sunday. Persuading non-believing

---

* Name changed for security reasons. In this book, we will refer to Barnabas' ministry as the HC Ministry (short for House Church Ministry).

campers to attend an evangelistic slide show was much easier than persuading them to listen to a sermon. It was a fun and effective way to make sure every camper who walked through the gates heard the gospel.

The camp used our slide show for more than ten years, and the feedback from the campers was great. I believed it helped them think about the meaning of life, and how God could be the answer to their salvation.

Margaret told me that if she dies before me, I am allowed to remarry. But I told her I will not do so. I don't want to try to please another woman. When you have the best, it's hard to accept the runners-up. I also believe Adam and Eve had one choice. There was no other man or woman around, and God did not give Adam a second woman. God wants me to have only one wife because He knows I cannot handle more than one in my lifetime. If Margaret goes before me, I will spend all my time with my ministry in China and not remarry. She is still the only one on my list; no other woman can take her place.

I read a short story where someone asked an old farmer in a small village what the difference was between love and marriage, thinking the farmer could not tell the difference. But the farmer was very wise. He said, "If you slept with her today, and tomorrow you still *want* to sleep with her, then it is love. If you slept with her today, and you still *have* to sleep with her tomorrow, then that is marriage." But I have my own understanding of the difference between love and marriage. Margaret and I have a good marriage, full of love. Of course, that doesn't mean we don't have ups and downs like every married couple. During the down times, I look first at my own behavior, my words, my attitude, and body language. I find I'm often the one who needs to say sorry and ask forgiveness from God and Margaret. Those times are the most difficult moments for me in our marriage, but I've learned to celebrate our differences, accept our imperfections, and trust God for a beautiful marriage.

For nearly forty years of marriage, I have learned that if a family has no love, it is not a family. Family is a place to learn how to love each other every day. Marriage is a God-given, lifetime assignment. It is a lifetime course, from which I will only graduate when I die. God didn't give me a pre-built family. He gave me the materials, and I have had to build my family. It has taken me my whole life to build my sweet home, and for me, it is still a work in progress.

Biblical love means to be respectful, to listen, and to accept my loved ones' ideas and opinions, even if they're different from mine. Biblical love is being willing to surrender yourself, and not caring who gets the credit, glory, or praise.

For the Love of my Life

The morning sun is roaming in the hazy colorful rain,

I am walking with you, my love, along in an ever-changing world.

I will not let go of your hand.

Please accept my imperfect love, continue to love me to the end.

Thank you.

10
I THOUGHT I COULD DO EVERYTHING

Fujian, China, 2000

During that nineteen-hour bus ride to Guangzhou, I had a lot of time for reflection. I knew I would learn from the mistakes I made. Ever since close calls in 1989 and 1993, I made sure none of my documents, whether printed or digital, said anything negative about the Chinese government. I also knew they had my name on file. While they allowed me into China, I had to be very careful every time. While I didn't fully understand Chinese politics at the time, I knew for sure the Chinese government was concerned about things they didn't understand, things they couldn't control, and things with an external influence. They talked about it in terms of stability, but it's basically control.

The Chinese government is determined to maintain control over social order, and to remain the dominant influence in their citizens' lives. Any force that might sway the hearts and minds of the people away from communist ideals is considered a major threat and a matter of national security. Christianity's growing number of believers is rapidly exceeding that of the Communist Party membership, and this makes government authorities nervous.

———————

Sun and I finally arrived in Guangzhou at 5:30 a.m. and met up with my two friends from the Hong Kong camp. We went to their hotel, where Sun and I could finally clean up and eat a full meal. However, we couldn't rest. We needed to meet the church sisters, get my permit, and then take the train to Hong Kong. We decided the Guangzhou airport would be the best place to meet, since the sisters would fly directly back to Fuzhou.

We went to the airport and met the sisters from Fuzhou who had my Home Return Permit. At the time, we did not know how it had been safely retrieved. But I learned that about 150 police officers, soldiers, and government officials had surrounded the house. (Months later, I learned that the twelve-year-old daughter had been in prison for three days. The mother, the house owner, had been imprisoned for three months, and tortured). Those who had fled were still on the run. I prayed and asked God to help them. I felt guilty that I brought suffering on them, but I received many phone calls from the other sisters in Fuzhou. They comforted me with kind words and prayers, wishing me safety on my return to Hong Kong and the U.S. (Five years later, I met the owner of the house in another province, and we had a good time encouraging each other).

———————————

I was deeply touched, and told God I was ready to do anything I could if God allowed. I was willing to help the house churches in China, even if I had to die. Yes, I was serious. God gave me all the courage I needed to face the situation. I knew this was not the most difficult challenge I would face. I learned from this special experience that having no power or ability to manage my own life is actually my greatest power and ability. When I had to run without my permit, I could only rely on my Lord to help me. I knew the most important reason for many of the churches to stay underground was their refusal to accept the state as their supreme authority of church affairs as dictated by the CCP. I agreed with the philosophy and beliefs of the underground churches, and I committed to serve them with all my heart. This full-time call went as far back as the night I was saved and called to serve the House Church.

Hong Kong, 1970s

By 1976, I felt it was time to go to seminary in order to become a full-time pastor. I applied and was accepted to the Christian Missionary Alliance seminary on Cheung Chau Island. However, I wanted to work at my church in Tai Po full-time for one year to earn practical experience before I started seminary. I had already pastored my church part-time since 1972 while I worked at the Christian camp, but I knew I needed more experience. So I quit working at the camp and began working full-time at my church with plans to begin seminary in the fall of 1977.

There were about 150 members in the church, but on an average Sunday, only fifty to eighty would actually attend the service. Our prayer meeting only had two or three people attending. It included a brief Bible study, but no one really seemed interested or eager to learn more about the Bible. They acted as if it was an obligation to come to church and that's all they had to do. If they just came to church, it was enough to make God happy.

I desperately wanted to change their attitudes. Hong Kong culture is a sophisticated mix of the East and the West. Hong Kong culture is quite different from the culture of mainland China, although the majority of Hong Kong citizens are ethnically Chinese. Hong Kong people are mainly from Southern China — Guangdong Province — and the language is Cantonese. Hong Kong people are open-minded, and we like to accept variety.

Hong Kong is one of the key financial centers of the world. China's companies use Hong Kong to access stock markets and Western capitalism. Hong Kong also values efficiency and making money. People work very hard and enjoy life in their limited free time after work.

What is Hong Kong's core value, and how does it affect the people in Hong Kong? Recently, I walked into a small barbershop in Hong Kong. It was a Wednesday evening around 7 p.m. Every Wednesday night and Sunday afternoon, the Hong Kong Royal Jockey Club, founded in 1844 by the British, provides an avenue for gambling on horse races. On gambling day, all the newspapers will have a few sections about horseracing. After I took my seat and the barber started to cut my hair, he asked me:

> *"Which horse did you choose for the first race tonight?"*

> *"I don't gamble."*

> *"Oh, gambling is important! If you do not gamble, how will you know when your luck comes to you? I like to gamble. I need money! I want to travel the world. Only gambling can help me achieve my goals in life, like buying a condo, traveling, and enjoying life!"*

I had no easy answer to his question.

Hong Kong people love three things: 1. Money, 2. Money, 3. Money.

Mainland Chinese are the same way. They are not interested in anything that cannot be turned into money.

One Sunday, after I had finished preaching, I was on the platform waiting for the light rail in Tuen Mun, Hong Kong. It was a small platform, and the only other people waiting for the rail were a mother and her son. Suddenly, I heard the mother speaking loudly to her son, who was about eight or nine years old:

> *"You are so stupid! Why do you want to take the 500 Hong Kong dollar bill you picked up from this platform to the police station? If you pick up something and no one is around, then it is yours."*

> *"No, mother. At school, our teachers teach us to be honest. If we pick something up that does not belong to us, then the best thing to do is take it to the police station."*

"No, give me the 500 dollars, you stupid kid. I'm unlucky to have given birth to you. I'd rather have given birth to a barbecued pork than have given birth to you!" (This is a Hong Kong idiom)

Proclaiming the gospel of Jesus Christ in a city that worships utilitarianism is very difficult. Utilitarianism opposes the sacrificial love of Jesus Christ. It is hard for Hong Kong people to believe someone would love them for no reason. Because they work so hard to make a living, they have no time for Jesus if He will not pay them. I think there are red Christians and golden Christians in both Hong Kong and China. Red Christians are those who follow the government more than they follow Jesus. Golden Christians are those who follow money and forget that our Lord provides for us. Hong Kong is a noisy city. My prayer for Hong Kong is, "Lord, we hear thousands of voices every day. May we hear Yours! Amen."

Even though I worked hard from the time I was five years old, I never had any money for myself. My mother took it all from me without providing enough food, clothing, or even love in exchange. Yet God always provided for me, even when I hated my adoptive mother, before I was a Christian, when I never wanted to be one.

Instead of money being the determining factor of success, I've always believed that giving is the thermometer of love. Giving money tests our love for God, because money is so important to our daily lives and future. Therefore, I give God the favorite things I love the most: usually my money and myself. Tithing is our contribution to God, He only asks us for 10 percent. My adoptive mother asked me for 90 percent, so I am willing to give more than 10 percent to my Lord.

Seeing God's provision even in my utter poverty gave me a crazy idea as I pastored my church. I wanted to teach them how to trust God, especially with money and material things. It was a small village church of poor people, who didn't have much to give. But I knew they loved money and material things, because when I was younger, they had made me steal and sell donated goods for money. Many people in the church did not tithe, and we barely survived year to year.

However, some years we had a tithe surplus, about 1,000 Hong Kong dollars, to carry over to the next year. In the mid-1970s, that was quite a large sum for a small church. But I decided to give away the surplus to other churches that were in financial need, and to the impoverished in our community. For two years, on January 1st, we started our books with zero funds. But the Lord blessed us and provided for us, just as we had provided for those in need around us.

Meanwhile, I tried to care for the church members and show them God's love. Most of them were older than I was, and they didn't necessarily recognize me as a pastor, or understand what Christian love was.

Most were uneducated, and about 70 percent were women, which was common for churches in Hong Kong during those days. They only saw me as a young man who would preach, and come to visit their boat or hospital when they were sick and pray with them. Not many people would choose to attend a church like that if they had a choice. But I didn't have a choice. Though I didn't like the church, the high ratio of women to men and the education level reflects the current demographics of the House Church in China today. Even then, God was preparing me to serve Him and the House Church.

I struggled with my sermons. I had no money to buy commentaries to learn more about the Bible, so I would visit the Christian bookstore and read in the store. I didn't understand many parts of the Bible. I would talk to other pastors, trying to find answers to difficult passages. However, I don't think they knew the answers themselves. They grew annoyed by my questions, seeing them as doubts about God. Some said I shouldn't even be a pastor, since I didn't have any formal training. I knew my sermons were boring. I struggled to explain the Bible, and had no funny stories to tell. I could see people fall asleep when I preached. But I kept working and preaching, confident in God and in what He was doing through me.

It was during this pastorate that I had my first encounter with demonic activity. Even at that time, fishing was a dying industry in Hong Kong. Fishermen used to live on their boats, but they had large families. The space was small, and their income was even smaller. The old way of life wasn't possible anymore. To solve this problem, the Hong Kong government built public housing for the fishermen and their families. They would have to live on dry land, but the quality of their life would improve.

There was one family who lived in the fishing village of San Men Zai. The older son Wan was my good friend, and their whole family attended my church. One day, Wan called me and told me that his grandmother had passed away. His whole family, including his grandmother, were sincere born-again Christians. Part of my pastoral responsibility was to visit the family and comfort them in their loss. I also needed to help them settle important matters and to officiate the funeral.

When I arrived at Wan's home, he told me that some strange things were happening in his home. There was a staircase in their house, and every time they walked up or down the stairs, they became weak and fainted. This had begun when their grandmother died. Her body was still in the home, lying in an open casket in the living room for the visitation. I was only twenty years old at the time, a young man still learning many things about the Bible and Christianity. I had no experience with demonic activity. However, I did know this was a true Christian family of eight suffering something real and spiritual in nature. I believed demonic activity and possession were real. There were many cases of demonic possession in the villages, because most people engaged in ancestor and idol worship, and even witchcraft.

I began to pray and walk up the steps. I wasn't fearful, but I knew I had to depend on God and His power. I prayed for wisdom and boldness. I also asked the family to pray. As I did,

I suddenly felt the Lord giving me insight that someone had left items related to witchcraft in the house, someone from outside the family who must have visited upon the grandmother's passing.

I started to look for the items. Under the stairs, I found something unusual. It was a fried egg on a plate. On top of the egg was a piece of rectangular yellow paper. Now, I wasn't sure if the egg or plate was important, but I did know the piece of paper was significant. This kind of paper is known as Joss paper and is still popular in Asian culture today, originating from a blend of Taoism and regional folklore. The little pieces of paper are used in ancestor worship, on important religious days, and at funerals. Joss paper is sometimes scattered around the grave or burned. Some believe the yellow color represents gold that the deceased can take into the afterlife in order to buy access to heaven. I took the Joss paper outside and burned it . . . not ceremoniously, but to get rid of it permanently.

However, the family was still affected by the stairs. So I began looking again. My thoughts turned to the body of the grandmother. I asked the family for their permission to search around her body. There I found two more pieces of yellow paper tucked into each of her sleeves. I burned these as well.

As the story began to spread around the village, it was discovered that, indeed, a relative who visited the family had secretly placed the items in their home. While he intended for them to be a blessing, he didn't realize he had actually brought a curse on the family.

Through that experience, the family grew in their faith. I also shared the gospel with the relative, and he became a Christian as well. It gave me valuable experience in spiritual warfare and demonic activity. I knew it was real, but I had never experienced it before like that. False religions are everywhere and their gods aren't real, but Satan uses them against God's people and the church. We can never dismiss superstitions as harmless. We must keep watch over the church and trust God when we encounter demonic activity.

I don't feel as though I did a very good job of pastoring my church, but there were some good changes. The youth fellowship grew, and I started two more youth fellowships for different age groups. However, the main church itself didn't grow as I had hoped, and the people didn't grow to love God as I prayed, so diligently, that they would.

However, those five years, from 1972 to 1977, including one year as full-time pastor, were so important in my life. God kept me humble. He didn't let the success of the growing youth fellowship or my evangelistic outreaches in the first two years of my Christian walk go to my head. At first, I thought I could do everything. This partly came from me wanting to prove myself. As an orphan, I wanted to prove to others that I mattered, I existed, and I was a good person. I may have seemed humble, but inside, I wanted to prove myself in every way to others. I wanted success in everything I did. But I learned I had to trust God, because no matter how hard I tried, nothing would succeed without Him.

I also learned to wait upon God. I didn't see much growth and had many difficulties, but I learned that everything is in God's hands. I needed to wait on His timing. His timing is better than mine, and I needed to understand His plan for my life. I learned that I shouldn't move unless my Lord tells me to move. Learning to walk after Him and letting Him lead the way is the meaning of following Jesus. I'm glad I learned to follow Jesus all the way. I never make important decisions for my own life until I seek and understand God's plan. I have seen miracle after miracle take place.

My yearlong full-time pastorate ended in the fall of 1977. I wanted to attend seminary, but the director of the Christian camp was leaving to earn his master's degree in the United States and asked me to serve as the acting director of the camp. He even offered to help me with my seminary education after he returned. I agreed, but sadly, his promise never materialized.

Ministry is incredibly difficult. Many pastors quit soon after their first full-time position, never to return. They become disillusioned by how they're treated, and their confidence is crushed when they fail to accomplish what they wanted. I wondered if I had made the right decision to pastor for one long, difficult year only to not go to seminary. I was also bitter because the promise to help me attend seminary never came true. But I learned one important lesson. If I do promise something, I must always keep that promise, and I will never promise what I cannot deliver.

My spiritual perspective about money is that I must trust my Lord's provision. Trust for me means that I do not care about how much money I have. I will soon marry my prince, Jesus Christ, and He owns the universe. I will spend time with Him in heaven, which has everything. So why should I worry about how much I have now? I have hope, and this hope is a promise from the most powerful God in the universe. He said He will keep His promises, so even if I have to suffer a little, it does not matter at all. I have a bright future. Some people are talented in investing and saving. However, I think loyalty to God is more important than any other talents or financial gains.

11

PREPARED TO TELL THE TRUTH

FUJIAN, CHINA, 2000

After I received my Home Return Permit at the Guangzhou airport, my two friends from the Hong Kong camp and I quickly left on the train for the Hong Kong border. We had been through so much in only two days. How could my thank you be sufficient to the two sisters and Sun, who had risked their freedom to bring me my permit?

They asked if I would come back. I told them I would. "We are disciples of Jesus," I said. "We must not be afraid to proclaim the truth. Our ability to overcome atheism will depend upon our insistence on the truth, and our bravery and courage to stand for our principles. We must not compromise the truth, surrender the truth, or betray the truth." I promised to pray for them every day in Hong Kong and overseas. I would try my best to tell Christians in Hong Kong, the U.S., and everywhere else to support the right of Chinese believers to practice their religion freely, without interference from atheist authorities. Prayer is very powerful, and it changes things.

We separated in the airport at 10:45 a.m., and the two camp staff members traveled with me for two hours by train to Shenzhen, where we would go through Chinese immigration into Hong Kong. When we arrived, I told them to stand in a separate line behind me so they would know what happened to me. If I was arrested, they could not help me, but they could at least return to Hong Kong and ask people to pray.

I stepped up to the immigration counter and handed the officer my Home Return Permit. I prayed silently. The officer looked at a big book in front of her, probably to check if my name was on the wanted list. She checked the book for a few minutes, longer than anyone who was before me, then looked up and stared at me. I had been through immigration many times, but I had never had an officer just stare at me for what seemed like minutes.

At last, she handed me my permit and motioned for me to go through. I took a deep breath of freedom as I passed into Hong Kong territory. It was exactly 1:30 p.m., forty-nine hours after I ran from the house.

———————————

Serving the House Church in China was far beyond my comfort zone. I knew that I would have to return to China, and I have many times, even to this day. Each time I returned, I would need to depend on God to protect me and to protect those whom I served. No matter how fearful I was of the authorities, I had to do what was right in God's eyes.

THE UNITED STATES, 1996

Margaret and I sat in the Buffalo, New York immigration office on a bitter-cold winter morning on January 2, 1996. We were from Hong Kong and still not used to cold weather. The immigration officer looked at the first page of my green card application. After reading for a couple of minutes, he asked me, "Mr. Young, are you the manager of this Chinese restaurant?"

I had come to the United States with my entire family to finish my education on a student visa. Now I had the opportunity to receive an American green card, a dream for countless immigrants. My lawyer had told me my only chance to obtain a green card was to lie that I was the manager of a Chinese restaurant. Now, as I looked back into the immigration officer's eyes, I knew I had to give him an answer.

———————————

In January 1995, after years of prayer, I really felt the Lord was leading me to leave the ministry of the Hong Kong Christian camp after twenty-three years. I needed to finish my education in order to equip myself for serving the House Church in China, which had been my firm calling since I was fifteen years old. That January, I gave the camp my six-month notice. The board asked me to stay, but my decision was made. Margaret supported me, and she knew my dream was to earn a degree in higher education.

I hadn't yet applied for colleges in the U.S. or seminary in Hong Kong, but I decided to trust my Lord to lead me. It was clear I needed to break out of my comfort zone. I had two sons who needed to go to school. If I stayed at the camp, I could have a comfortable life, but if I quit, I would have a lot of uncertainty. However, I trusted the Lord to lead me. I wanted to experience His provision through His guidance. Hong Kong and the United States were both options for my studies, but it would be difficult for me to go to the States because I didn't have enough money for a student visa. If I studied in Hong Kong, I could go to The Christian and Missionary Alliance Seminary.

Camp-of-the-Woods, which sponsored my 1980 trip to Wisconsin, had also invited my family to spend time at the camp during the summers of 1992, 1993, and 1994. The camp had a regular morning chapel service and I was invited to speak for a few minutes about the Christian camp in Hong Kong. There I met Dr. John Van Wicklin, a professor at Houghton College. I would meet with John after chapel at the snack shop, where we got to know each other. In 1994, my last summer at the camp, I told him God had called me to work with the House Church in China and I wanted to earn my seminary degree from a university in Hong Kong. He asked me if I had thought about studying in the United States. I said I had, but I didn't tell him that I didn't have the money to move or attend school. I also had to think about my family, visas, entrance exams, and applications. It was a big decision, and at that time, I felt it was too difficult. But he wanted to help me attend Houghton College. At his urging, I wrote him a letter in February of 1995 expressing my desire to attend Houghton College. In March, I received his reply that I had been accepted at the school. It was my responsibility to fill out and submit all the correct paperwork, but he would help me through the process.

The same year, in April, I was invited by the American Baseball Coaches Association in the United States to attend a baseball sports ministry training in Chicago with Tom Roy of Unlimited Potential as my host. I had a great time at the training, and afterward on my way back to Hong Kong, I stopped in Los Angeles to visit my friends Danny and Connie. They had formerly worked at the Christian camp in Hong Kong and knew my dream to study in the United States.

Danny and Connie told me that Hong Kong citizens were eligible to apply for the U.S. green card lottery, so there was a chance I could get a green card more easily. As a conservative Christian, the word "lottery" didn't seem spiritual, but I understood it was the system. It was difficult for anyone to get a U.S. green card. Even people with millions of dollars still had to wait ten years for their application to be approved. However, my friend convinced me it was worth a try.

The application for the green card lottery system was quite simple. My friend wrote my name, address, and phone number on the back of a white envelope, and told me all I need to do is write my Hong Kong ID number, and then take the envelope back to Hong Kong and mail it to the United States, since it had to be mailed from my home country. So I brought it back to Hong Kong, mailed it, and then forgot about it. I didn't even tell Margaret about it.

Meanwhile, I applied for my student visa at the U.S. Embassy in Hong Kong, as well as for permission to bring my wife and two sons. I took the TOEFL test, an English proficiency test to ensure non-native English speakers can succeed in school or work. I earned a very high score, but I knew I didn't have enough money to prove I could afford four years of full-time study with my family. Still, I filled out all the forms, obtained the necessary recommendations, college paperwork, and other required supporting documentation. On May 25, 1995, I went to the U.S. Embassy in Hong Kong for my student visa interview.

Margaret and I arrived early, so we were the first couple to be interviewed. We were directed to the interview room, where two consulate officers were ready to interview us. One was a manager, and the other was a trainee. When Margaret and I sat down, the manager examined the first page of my application. I had placed my financial documents in the middle of the stack of documents, hoping the officer might not pay much attention to them. Without addressing Margaret or me, the manager said to the trainee, "Look, this guy is already thirty-nine years old. I'm sure he's saved enough money to be a freshman in college, unlike the high school students who only go to make their parents happy. At his age, he knows why he wants to be a student."

Without asking us any questions or reading through my documents, she stamped "approved" on my application form and gave me a receipt. She said, "Come back tomorrow at 4 p.m. to pick up your passport. Your student visa for the whole family will be granted to you. Congratulations, Mr. Young!"

When God paves the way, no one can stop things from happening. This was an amazing experience for my family and me. Margaret and I were so happy, and we went for a nice lunch to celebrate. I left Hong Kong on July 25, 1995 with my family to enroll as a freshman at Houghton College in upstate New York.

College started in late August. Not only did I study, but I also worked in the kitchen, and as a security guard. Margaret also worked at the cafeteria making salads. In the summer, Americans want cold drinks with lots of ice, but Margaret would drink hot tea, as is the custom for most Asians. It was hard for Margaret's American colleagues to understand, and they would always ask her, "How can you drink hot tea in such hot weather?" We both had to adjust to a completely different culture and language far from home. It wasn't easy, as anyone who has lived overseas would know, but we kept each other strong.

I was thirty-nine when I started as a freshman at Houghton. I was much older than my classmates. I still remember during my first month at college, when my son's classmates asked him, "What subject does your father teach at the college?" My son, eleven years old at the time, said, "My father is a freshman at the college. He is not a professor!"

Our first Sunday at Houghton, I attended the Wesleyan church. After the worship and opening prayer, the pastor introduced the Sunday school teachers for each grade, because it was the end of summer break. I couldn't believe my eyes. Not only were half of the teachers men, but they were all professors, PhDs. Some of the female teachers were also professors. This usually never happens in Hong Kong and Chinese churches. Ninety-nine percent of Sunday school teachers are women. Teaching is not viewed as important as being a deacon, doing administrative work, or making important decisions—responsibilities that are given to educated men. What a difference in culture, even in Christian culture. I liked the American culture. It is biblical, and all men and women are created equal.

By the last week of September, after one month of college, I received a package from the Christian camp in Hong Kong. Without knowing the contents, they had mailed it to me using the slowest delivery option. When I opened it, I found some very important documents.

I had won the green card lottery.

But because of the time it took the camp to ship my documents, I only had four days to complete the paperwork and send it to the Buffalo immigration office. I consulted the lawyer of my friend Danny in Los Angeles. He helped me with some ideas, and sent me an employment letter from a Chinese restaurant, which was a five-hour drive away from Houghton. The lawyer said, "You'll definitely need this. Just tell the immigration office you're the manager of this Chinese restaurant."

"Oh . . ." was my only reaction on the phone.

Margaret and I walked into the Buffalo, New York immigration office on January 2, 1996. The officer and I greeted each other. We sat down, and he looked at the first page of my application. After reading for a couple of minutes, he asked me, "Mr. Young, are you the manager of this Chinese restaurant?" Now, having a forty-hour-a-week job was a requirement for a green card and I knew this at the time. However, the officer knew that the restaurant was more than a five-hour drive away from Houghton College, and that it was impossible for me to attend school and work a full-time job so far away.

But I had prepared myself to tell the truth. I knew he would ask me this question. Although the lawyer told me to lie, I knew I could not. God did not want me to lie. He wanted me to depend on Him. So I answered with great confidence, "No, sir, to tell you the truth, I am not working at this restaurant. I don't even know where it is. I'm a full-time student at Houghton College and work for twenty hours on campus, which is the maximum amount I can work as an international student. One of my friend's lawyers, who is also Chinese, sent me this letter from the restaurant. It isn't right to lie to you, but I didn't want to take this letter away. I wanted to have a chance to explain it to you. Thank you for giving me the time to explain this to you, sir!"

The officer looked at me in silence, but then suddenly, his eyes lit up. He smiled, saying, "Mr. Young, I admire your honesty. Usually, people come to my office for immigration interviews and lie to me. They say things that are hard for me to believe, and make up crazy reasons to convince me to give them the green card. I wondered if you were being honest with me or playing tricks, but I know you're honest."

He continued, "Mr. Young, this restaurant is the only proof of full-time work you have, which is a requirement for a green card. Though you don't have a forty-hour weekly job, you do work hard for twenty hours as a student, and you're honest. Therefore, I'm going to grant you the green card for your family, and you can work more hours now if the college has a job for you. Mr. Young, congratulations! You state here you want your American name to be 'Barnabas'?"

"Yes, sir!" I replied to the officer with a great smile, and Margaret, next to me, was joyful too. I thank God He gave me the courage to tell the truth. It seemed as though I had no chance for a green card if I told the truth about my lack of employment, but the Lord made a way, and the officer gave me the green card.

All my friends thought I must have been planning for this a long time, because no one could possibly get a green card so easily and honestly. But I had never even considered getting a green card. I was just happy to get my student visa, so I could come to United States with my family.

————————

After we successfully applied for our green cards, I was able to work more hours as a resident alien of the United States. So from my second semester onward, I dropped my cafeteria job, and increased my hours as a security guard. In fact, I remained a security guard throughout my student years at Houghton. I even went back to work at Houghton after I started my MBA at Rochester Institute of Technology. I had been trained and passed a simple exam to become a licensed security guard of the New York State.

I worked the night shift three to four times each week, typically from 9 p.m. to midnight. I would be responsible for closing and locking buildings at 11 p.m., as well as closing windows and asking students to leave the buildings. At least two nights per week, I would have to work from 9 p.m. to 3 a.m., and then go to class at 8 a.m. that same morning.

Houghton has a small campus, and night shifts were quiet in terms of incidents. I was often responsible for helping professors and students retrieve their car keys from their (accidentally) locked cars and make sure buildings were locked up at the proper times. This gave me downtime to study for my classes. I was able to fulfill all of my duties and study in peace, so the job suited me well.

There were some dramatic scenarios as a security guard, despite Houghton being such a small college. One night I was doing my normal patrol around campus, when I thought I saw something out of the ordinary off a hiking path. I walked up to look in the woodlands that surrounded the college. I found a girl whose attacker I had frightened off when I approached them. She had gone out for an evening jog on the secluded path at dusk, when a man grabbed her and attempted to rape her. I helped her out of the woods and called the police for her.

Another time, I was alerted to the presence of marijuana smoke and the sounds of a male voice coming from one of the female dorms, which was not allowed. I went over to the dorm, where several female students were already waiting for me. They told me they had discovered a boy hiding in one of the dorm rooms because a female student had invited him over. The students who called me knocked on the door while I stood guard (because it would have been awkward if I were the one to knock). When the door opened, the girls scouted out the room, noticed the female resident sitting there, and asked me to come in. I immediately saw someone crouching (and clearly hiding) by the closet, and sure enough, it was the boy.

I asked him to leave the room and go into the lounge area. He complied without incident. He also had a backpack with him.

The girl was nervous and didn't say anything. We all thought that the girl was the one who invited the boy into her room, but that didn't seem to be the case upon later investigation. The boy was the son of a German diplomat from New York City and knew the girl. He had come to try to sell drugs to her. I knew I could not handle this matter on my own, and probably needed to phone the police. However, I still wanted to be sure if the drug allegation was valid. When I asked the boy what he had inside his backpack, he didn't respond.

I asked him again, "I'm sorry, but there are rules at this college that prohibit men from entering this dormitory during non-visiting hours. You are not allowed to be here, and I have received reports of you engaging in illicit behavior. I would like to check your backpack."

"I do not want to show you," he replied. These are my private belongings, and it's a private matter." As soon as he said that, I knew I had three options: let him go, call my security supervisor, or call the police.

As I was pondering my next steps, I saw him quietly reach inside his bag for something. I immediately grabbed his hand and the bag. I felt a piece of metal inside. Sure enough, once I opened the bag, I saw a gun inside.

I kept him restrained as best I could, and asked one of the girls to call the police immediately, as well as my supervisor Ray. Once Ray was informed, he gathered a group of staff members to come help me restrain the boy. The police arrived, took my statement, and then took the boy away.

I was very thankful to God; the boy could have fought me if he wanted to. There were no guarantees I could have kept him restrained. He could have been much more aggressive and beat me to the punch—figuratively and literally. It could have been much worse, and I'm very grateful to the Lord that the incident was peacefully resolved.

However, I'm most thankful to the Lord for preparing me, even in my security job, to serve the House Church. My family and I had never lived in a location that cold before, and it required many adjustments on our part. When I started working more hours at security, it was January, the dead of winter in western New York. The job required a lot of walking outside in the snow *at night*, something I had never really done. I slipped on the snow many times and had to walk in and out of buildings, struggling with coats, jackets, and scarves I had never needed to wear before. I also had never driven in the snow, and it took me a year before I could drive the college-owned security vehicles. Overall, the Lord used that experience to train and prepare me, because He would soon send me to many rural Chinese villages in midwinter to visit homes and churches with little to no heat for days on end.

I didn't receive my bachelor's degree until 1999, when I was forty-three years old. Although I had been doing well in ministry, I felt as though some people looked down on me because of my lack of education. Perhaps they did not feel that way, but it was always a struggle for me. I prayed and asked God why they treated me as if I were less than them. I was living under my society's standard that if you don't have a college degree, you're not good enough. Without a degree, one could only do certain kinds of work, not receive much pay, and not be promoted. I knew I should focus my eyes on Jesus, but Jesus was invisible and I was in the visible world. So sometimes, my worldview was not a kingdom worldview. I cared about myself too much. However, God knew I needed many years of spiritual training before working on my higher education. His training humbled me.

After five years with a green card, I had the opportunity to become an American citizen. I answered yes. So my whole family became American citizens. My oldest son was about to turn eighteen when we received our citizenship. If he had turned eighteen before his citizenship was approved, he would have had to apply for citizenship on his own. We praised the Lord for helping our family receive U.S. citizenship, so we could work and study in the U.S. I went on to receive an MBA from the Rochester Institute of Technology. Then in August 2000, we returned to serve the House Church in China.

Benjamin Franklin, a founding father of the United States, said, "Where liberty is, there is my country." I am a citizen of God's kingdom. I have an American passport, and I love the United States. I do not like the Chinese Communist Party, and will not, unless they repent and make changes, but I love China and serve the house churches of China. They are God's people, and I love them. I have devoted my life to serve them, and I am willing to be in prison or even die for the gospel, like many of my Chinese pastor friends. Our Lord Jesus is the one we serve.

I know whom I serve, and I also know my opposition. I have served in Chinese student university groups in the United States. Whenever I talked about persecution of pastors in China, a few students would stand up and angrily leave the room. But China belongs to the Chinese people. It does not belong to the Chinese Communist Party. As in the United States, America belongs to the American people, not to the Republicans or the Democrats. No one can stop me from telling the truth.

Martin Luther King said, "Cowardice asks the question, 'Is it safe?' Expediency asks the question, 'Is it politic?' Vanity asks the question, 'Is it popular?' But conscience asks the question, 'Is it right?' There comes a time when one must take a position that is neither safe, nor politic, nor popular, but one must take it because one's conscience says that it is right."

God tells me to do the right thing. If I don't understand how the house church pastors suffer for our Lord, I do not know the love of Jesus Christ. If I choose not to serve the house church pastors because I am afraid of suffering, I do not deserve the love of Jesus Christ. God will give me the strength to serve. I am not going to just end up on someone's prayer list. I am going to fight the good fight on the front line. I have the presence of my Lord with me wherever I go. All glory to God.

12

GOING UNDERGROUND

CENTRAL CHINA, 2000

I received a call in April 2000, just a week before Easter. A Canadian had started an NGO to support persecuted Christians throughout the world, including house church Christians in China. He asked me to go to Burma with him for a week to meet with the head of a large Chinese house church movement and other house church leaders. I was still in the MBA program at RIT, and I would be completing my degree in a few weeks. I told him it was an inconvenient time, because I would need to take time off from my studies to go to Burma. He agreed to change the meeting location to China, because he knew of a four-day house church training, which was taking place at a facility that was literally underground. He offered for me to be a speaker at that training. Since I was called to China and had this opportunity, I took it without hesitation.

This was my first visit to central China, and only a few months before my forty-nine-hour escape from Fujian Province. This was also my first time working with the House Church movement, so I wasn't sure what to expect. I didn't even speak Mandarin yet, only Cantonese and English.* It was dangerous. There was always the possibility of the police finding us. We had to be careful, ensure we weren't followed, and meet in secret locations.

I found myself packed into a tiny room with about one hundred house church pastors starving for biblical teaching. They had no seminary training or Bible study books. They were eager to learn, and asked me to teach from early in the

---

* Cantonese is the official language of Hong Kong. Mandarin is the official language of mainland China. Both use Chinese characters for writing, but Hong Kong uses traditional characters, while mainland China uses simplified characters.

morning to late in the evening, with only a few short breaks for meals.

The largest Three-Self seminary in all of China is Nanjing Union Theological Seminary. Its teaching is theologically liberal and heretical in some ways. It is also tightly controlled by both the CCP and the China Christian Council, a government executive committee that oversees all Protestant churches, seminaries, and Bible distribution in China. There are another ten smaller government-run seminaries as well. While China points to the existence of these undergraduate seminaries to claim that religious freedom is allowed, they are actually small, tightly-controlled programs. Some are not necessarily engaged in solid biblical teaching, and instead propagate communist agendas. While many dedicated Christian pastors have graduated from these seminaries and serve the Lord, some feel they cannot attend with a clear conscience. Others who are called to be pastors may not have the finances to attend, or cannot move where the seminaries are located. If they are young, they may not be able to enroll openly due to family conflicts.

Most pastors in China have limited access to concordances, theological dictionaries, commentaries, and other Bible study aids. It is also difficult for them to access Bible software or online material due to the tightly controlled, censored, and monitored Chinese internet, known as "The Great Firewall." But their desire to learn about Jesus and the Bible is unquenchable. They pour over Scripture, learning all they can. Students study the entire Bible, but they place a special emphasis on the four Gospels because, as one leader said, "Jesus is the greatest example. His life teaches the students how to prepare a sermon and how to preach. His examples teach them how to live, how to suffer, and how to die."

Because of the issues surrounding Three-Self government seminaries, there are many secret Bible schools and training centers across China run by the House Church movement, like the one I was speaking at that day. These schools operate in order for students to learn the Bible without the influence of the CCP. Conditions vary greatly in training centers. Some Bible schools have been literally underground, in hand-dug facilities, but most are in non-descript buildings in both urban and rural areas. To avoid detection by local villagers and government officials, students at these locations rarely venture outside. These young people are often confined to their tight, dark quarters for months at a time in order to not draw the attention of the police. Candlelight sometimes provides the only form of illumination. Running water and toilets are often unavailable or very rudimentary. The students survive on simple food like mantou (steamed Chinese buns), vegetables (when available), and rice or noodles, which are provided by the local church if funds are available. The food is often delivered at night. Men and women sleep in separate sections of the space, sometimes on bare sand or a muddy ground. In rural locations, they often lack pillows and blankets and use only a layer of hay for warmth and comfort.

Today, a larger number of rural Bible schools operate in the homes of willing host families, or in barns or other vacant buildings donated by believers (often business people) for use as training centers. At these locations, conditions are far better. Some may not have heat, but electricity and sanitation facilities are available. Men and women sleep in separate rooms on floor mats, usually with quilts and pillows.

Urban underground Bible schools are often located in apartments, where up to thirty students can attend each six-month session. Schools may be male or female exclusively due to the confines of space. The apartments are located in the residential outskirts of larger cities. Students must limit their movements in and out of their schools, because foot traffic within the densely populated neighborhoods could easily arouse suspicion. As a result, students live and study inside their small living space for prolonged periods. Once every few weeks, some of them may be allowed to cautiously visit local shops to purchase necessary supplies.

After four days of teaching in a little room, we decided we needed to move to a different location and teach for two more days. My translator and I awoke at 4 a.m. and traveled through the pre-dawn darkness to reach the new meeting place. We not only had to avoid the secret police, but also the prying eyes of villagers who might notify the authorities if they saw something out of the ordinary. Worship and prayer began at 7 a.m., and I began teaching at 8 a.m.

At 8:15 a.m., I heard a loud voice urgently call out, "Run! The police are coming! We only have a couple minutes!" I ran outside and looked down the dirt road. Sure enough, I could see at least four government vehicles in the distance racing directly toward us. They had found us. We had to run.

A pastor I had just met for the first time implored me, "Teacher, we can't wait! We have to run now! I'll help you escape!"

We had no car or motorbikes. It was my first time to that area, so I had no idea where to go. The pastor began to run, and I followed him as he told me to do. For the next nine hours we ran. I lost count of how many mountains we climbed up and down. We walked through flooded rice paddies and had to lie down in the mud and water to avoid being spotted. But we pushed through, eventually finding our way to a small city and a place of safety by 7 p.m. that night.

This was my introduction to serving the House Church in China. I didn't know it at the time, but it was also a job interview.

UNITED STATES, 2000

After this trip to China, the Canadian offered me a job in Frisco, Texas, where they had established their U.S. headquarters. This was a big answer to prayer. I was fast approaching the completion of my degree, and Margaret and I had many questions as we pondered our next steps. The job offer gave us great clarity and reassurance at a time of uncertainty. My family could remain in the States while I traveled back and forth from China, doing the work I was called to do.

I joined the NGO as China Director in August of 2000, and began to develop a strategy to meet the needs of the House Church in China. I traveled into China almost monthly to meet with house church leaders, cultivate relationships, conduct teaching, and distribute aid as needed.

This was a daunting task to say the least. I was not from mainland China, and had yet to learn the culture. I didn't speak Mandarin, nor was I actually stationed in China. At the time, I also didn't have any strong connections to leaders within the House Church movement. How could I earn the trust of the house church leadership, who are secretive by necessity?

My April trip had already answered that question. I later learned I had earned the trust of that particular house church movement. I had taught from early in the morning to late at night for five days. This was typical of Bible school students and pastors-in-training in China. They rise every morning, seven days a week, at 5:00 a.m. The first two hours of their day are devoted to prayer, followed by an hour of worship. Breakfast is shared around 8:00 a.m. The students then participate in lectures and in-depth Bible study until lunchtime. During the late 1980s and early 1990s, students often had to skip lunch due to the severe lack of funds, but the situation is now improving. After lunch, students participate in further training sessions until 6:00 p.m., when they break for dinner. In the evening, there are more lectures or personal study time, Scripture memorization, and reflection until bedtime at roughly 10:00 p.m.

During this exhausting schedule, I made every effort to listen to each pastor who needed to talk with me personally. The pastors in China want to talk a lot about the difficulties in their lives, and ask many theological and biblical questions, almost non-stop. They're lonely, because they don't have many opportunities to interact with other pastors, to share their burdens, and to pray for one another. Trust is also an issue, because they cannot talk to the congregation. Even if they have the chance to talk to another pastor, they might fear that their secrets will leak out. In China, when I talk to one pastor, the others who are waiting in line will come as close as possible to listen to our conversation. So when I say I made "every effort," I really mean it.

On a later trip, I heard someone say to me:

> *"Hello, Teacher An* (my Chinese nickname)*, I'm so happy to finally have a chance to talk to you one-on-one. I have been waiting for this opportunity for three days! Praise the Lord! Praise the Lord!"*

He was so happy, looking at me with a big smile on his face. I knew I couldn't ignore him or refuse to talk to him.

> *"Hi, pastor. What is your name? It is nice to meet you."*

> *"My spiritual name is Heavenly Peace, I am from Inner Mongolia. I took a forty-eight-hour train ride to come here to attend your training, so it's nice to see you teacher. Praise our Lord!"*

Wow, this was an incredible story to hear deep in the heart of China during an underground Bible seminar. The only problem was it was 12:30 in the morning. We were face-to-face as I squatted over a hole-in-the-ground toilet with him beaming a flashlight at my face.

I had been invited to teach in an underground training center, which was underneath a small village house, accessed with a hidden tunnel. I walked down to find about one hundred Chinese pastors waiting to hear me teach for the next five days.

This was a literal cave. The walls were dirt and the ceiling was low. It had been hand-dug by the local Christians. Women slept in one room, while men slept in another. The main classroom had a handful of plastic stools, but most of the pastors had to sit on the dirt floor.

The toilet was a true Chinese toilet—a hole in the ground. It was uncovered, with no walls around it. No toilet bowl and no water. This is what all the toilets were like in China at the time, and these are still common in villages. When I was a boy, I was used to this type of toilet, because it was the same kind used in the poor fishing villages of Hong Kong in the 1960s and 1970s. But I wasn't used to it anymore, and was overcome with stench.

For the first two days, I avoided using the toilet except to pee. On the third night, I couldn't avoid it. I waited until eleven o'clock, then midnight. I checked every fifteen minutes, but pastors were still using the toilet. Finally, at 12:30 a.m. the last pastor had finished. I was so thankful to finally have a chance to relieve myself in private. Suddenly, the bright white beam of Pastor Heavenly Peace's flashlight lit me up mid-squat, with my pants around my ankles.

He squatted in front of me and after he introduced himself, I said to him:

> *"Pastor Heavenly Peace, praise the Lord that He brought us together. You made a big effort to come here. May our Lord richly bless you!"*

> *"Teacher An, I came to see you for a reason. I have a theological question that I want to ask. When a man receives Christ, is he once saved, always saved?"*

I tried my best to get back my privacy so I could finish up.

> *"Pastor Heavenly Peace, may we talk about this question tomorrow? I'm sure I will answer you, but maybe it's better to talk about this question with all the pastors together. I know you want to spend special time with*

me, and I promise you, I will spend time with you after
dinner. Is this okay?"

But Pastor Peace persisted:

"No, no, it is very hard for me to meet a good teacher!
Please, please share with me your wisdom from our Lord,
even for five minutes, please!"

I knew I couldn't say no again. For the next ten minutes while
I was squatting, I answered his questions. He received his
answer, and I once again had a little privacy.

This was a very special experience for me, to teach theology while
I was in such a situation. I knew I always had to be prepared to
give a defense, to teach, and to encourage. But I never knew I
had to be prepared while going to the bathroom. Believe it or
not, this has happened several times during my work in China.

I worked with the Christian NGO for eight years, building
connections gradually from one house church movement to
twenty-eight. We financially supported fourteen movements,
while maintaining relationships with another fourteen. Before,
I had waited for my phone to ring. Now, I couldn't wait for
my phone to stop ringing! We were funding Bible schools,
Bible printing, church planters, pastoral support, and more. I
was often the only connection to the outside world for these
house church movements, particularly the smaller ones, so I
brought them greetings and encouragement from Christians
around the world. I served as confidant and counselor to
many house church leaders, because their leadership roles and
culture placed great parameters on how they could express
themselves. Once I listened to their needs, I would report back
to the NGO, where the level of financial aid would be assessed.
Then I would travel back to China to distribute the funds, and
check how the previous funds had been used.

There was no way to transfer funds to a bank account, or to
have the churches send me photos of purchased materials or
Bibles. I had to personally travel to China and see for myself

everything that was being done. Then I would write up reports, ensuring the accountability of these operations to our donors.

I was very happy to be working with the House Church and fulfilling the call God had placed on my life. And overall, I was happy with the NGO. I was promoted to International Director in 2007. This was a blessing, and God used the organization to accomplish many great things around the world, and specifically for the House Church in China. But it is important to remember that while ministries and Christian organizations are generally led by Christians who hold to a Christian ethic, Christians are imperfect. Christian leaders can be susceptible to pride, greed, and even arrogance. As I have written before, I have learned from good bosses and bad bosses. I learn what to do and what not to do. And it is an important principle I want to share with you: hold yourself to a biblical ethic no matter the situation, and learn what you can from good and bad leaders.

In July of 2008, I began a new role as an independent contractor with the NGO, as opposed to a full-time employee. This was a much better situation for me. I also invited the founder of the Christian camp in Hong Kong, John Bechtel, to serve as a special advisor for the NGO. John had retired a couple of years earlier from a foundation in the United States, where he worked for twenty-three years.

I continued with the NGO for another year, but the new president brought new problems. He was a Ph.D. scholar, a professor in university, and the CEO of a big relief NGO, and he made sure everyone knew it. He brought up his academic credentials often and placed great faith in his abilities due to them. He disregarded others whom he didn't consider as educated as himself.

We had a relatively significant meeting at a hotel in Guilin, China. It was significant because it was the first time I was able to invite some top leaders from various Chinese house church movements to meet with our North American partners. We went to Guilin specifically because it was a popular tourist spot for both domestic and foreign tourists and was, therefore, a bit more under the radar. As we were discussing cross-cultural ministry, he stood up and said, "In order to do cross-cultural ministry, you *must* have PhDs." I couldn't believe he had said that, and because I was the translator, I chose not to translate it. Even our United States partners who were present were quite shocked at his hubris.

Another time, at a full-staff meeting, he said that the organization must keep two million U.S. dollars in reserves for staff salaries and headquarters upkeep. I immediately challenged him because our donors would not know about this, and would expect most of their donations to go directly into the mission field. I didn't think we even had two million dollars in our reserves.

Later, even though I was an independent contractor with the organization, he repeatedly demanded I return to a full-time position. This would have prevented me from working with other organizations, a precondition for my work. After this, I knew I had to leave the organization. I didn't know how I would continue my work with the House Church. I thought of all my brothers and sisters in China who depended on our relationship and help. I worried about the schools, churches, and families. I also didn't know how I would support my family. I needed to earn a salary or raise funding to support my family, as well as care for the House Church. I also knew God was leading me in a new direction, and I had to step out in faith. When I knew my time at the NGO was ending, I began to consider starting my own NGO for the House Church in China. In a conversation with John Bechtel and my sons, my older son suggested the name "HC Ministry*," which we agreed upon.

Some close friends of mine offered immediate support when they learned I had to resign. This was the beginning of the HC Ministry.

---

* Name changed for security reasons. In this book, we will refer to Barnabas' ministry as the HC Ministry (short for House Church Ministry).

13
WITHOUT FEARS OR WORRY

I was in love with Margaret from the first time we met at the Christian camp in Hong Kong. She became my partner not only in life, but also in ministry. She stepped out with me in faith every time we needed to. She encouraged me to earn my master's degree, traveled with me to China to serve as translator as I learned Mandarin, and began her own business to help the women of the House Church. She also volunteered her time and effort to help with building projects, including the layout for our office in Hong Kong, and the architectural design for our training facility in Asia. She did all this while raising our two sons, especially from 1985 to 1991 as I was working at least fourteen hours a day with the camp ministry. Her understanding and support has been a blessing to the ministry and me.

When I was with the NGO in Dallas, I needed a legitimate business platform to operate in China. In 2001, a group of house church pastors' widows heard that Margaret was an excellent seamstress and an arts and crafts enthusiast. They wanted to meet Margaret and learn more about arts and crafts. Margaret had been considering what her role might be alongside me for quite some time. She had never considered her hobby to be critical for my work in China, but her abilities were well received by the widows, and she promised to help their situation in any way she could.

We then established a social entrepreneurship specializing in handmade gifts. The system was simple: Margaret would train a group of urban house church women to prepare various kits to be mailed out to our rural house church women. The rural women would complete the items and mail them back to the urban women, where quality control inspections would be conducted. The products would then be shipped and sold in North America, with the profits contributing directly to the workers' wages. We were primarily interested in supporting rural local pastors, who otherwise would be forced to take on part-time work, and would be unable to minister full-time. Through providing their wives and relatives with work in their own home, they don't need to travel to other cities for work. These ladies can tend to their families while maintaining a flexible work schedule. This also provided me with a fitting platform in rural areas I would otherwise have no reason to be in ("Oh, I'm just out here to check on my workers!").

In 2005, Margaret discovered she had ovarian cancer. Her initial reaction was that it was better for her to have cancer than me, because I knew how to fill out all the medical forms and take care of her. She asked me if I was worried about her cancer. That was a hard question for me. If I said I wasn't worried, then it would seem as if I didn't care. I was concerned, but we both had great faith in God. Fear and worry is a great weapon of Satan. I had seen the faith of the house church pastors in China. They showed no fear when they faced great persecution. We knew to give thanks to the Lord in all circumstances.

Below are my writings during that time:

———————————

March 4

Dear coworkers, brothers, and sisters in Christ, thank you for your prayers.

Two weeks ago, Margaret felt something strange on her body as we got ready for our trip to China from Hong Kong. She did not feel pain or discomfort, but we scheduled a doctor's appointment for when we returned to Hong Kong.

On March 1 in the afternoon, Margaret went to her appointment and found out that she needed to have an hour-long procedure, which would require the doctors to anaesthetize her whole body to diagnosis the tumor as endometrial carcinoma. Yesterday, Margaret had the procedure. The results came this evening, and Margaret has to have a hysterectomy. The operation will be on March 9 at 10:45 a.m. and will take three hours with two doctors and one anesthetist. Further treatment could be needed if the tumor has spread to other parts of her body. The recovery period is four to six weeks and Margaret will need to stay in hospital for five days. No May trips will be affected at all at this moment.

Spiritually, Margaret and I are uplifted by prayer, and we do not have any hard feelings at all. We did not ask why. Instead, we just ask the Lord to give us the strength to go through it. We believe that our cross will not be greater or heavier than our Lord's grace. The sky is not blue all the time. Our Lord takes and gives. We trust our Lord will not turn His eyes away from us. We have eternal life through Jesus, so we will not be separated. We will not let Satan stop our ministry. We are cool and calm to fight a good fight. The battlefield now comes to our doorstep, so we are on the defense. Nothing can stop us from the love of our Lord, and we are going to trust Him and continue with our ministry until we see Him in heaven. We have committed to serve Him and nothing will make us turn back. The cup is bitter, but Jesus put some sugar in it, so it is sweet with Jesus as the ingredient. We will live up to what the Bible teaches us to be. We will continue to witness the power of God in this world. We can smile in the great thunderstorms when Jesus is with us on the boat, and He is with us right now. We have no fear, and we will not be powerless. Nothing will stop us unless the Lord tells us to rest. Sorry, I am not preaching, but this is what we believe. I know the power can only come from above, and my eyes are always looking up to Him these days.

When I will be in the hospital with Margaret next week for

five days, the hospital will be my office, and the ministry will continue. The battle is not over. I believe our suffering brothers and sisters still need us. I will be careful not to get sick, and I will eat something I like to release my pressure. Margaret needs me, and I will give her my greatest support, my time, and my strength in the Spirit.

We are fine, and we trust the Lord, we have you, and we have the Lord, that is enough.

Thank you again for your prayers

Your invisible brother,

B

———————————

Margaret wrote:

I have made some discoveries about myself. I am an incredibly optimistic person but a silly one at the same time. For example, consider my current condition. No matter what the doctor tells me, I can only analyze my situation through the simplest frame of mind. Although the facts from my latest development aren't as simple, happiness still runs through my veins. I think this type of attitude fits me well since I was never one to over-worry. After all, anxiety and melancholy only generate additional nuisance.

Perhaps this is a sign, a sign I need to change my mindset. I think God is trying to tell me something. Maybe He is trying to tell me that my sky won't always be blue, that my flowers won't always blossom. I am clueless about what He has planned for me. I was shocked when the doctors told me about my condition. I was able to accept it. I did not have worries, I was not frightened, and I was at peace. I immediately thought about the people in my life. My husband, he has the ability find another wife. My children, they are grown-up and independent. My parents are of no worry. I thought about my business, but that also is worry-free because God is in control. He is the navigator.

I have always prepared myself for tragedy though I have no clue how I'll react when the moment comes. Today I am not asking for God's help. Instead, I choose to obey His plan, and I will prepare myself.

I can say that I am a strange person, and Barnabas can testify to that. I am a private person, I don't like attention, and I don't seek sympathy. I didn't want to tell others about my condition. I didn't want to bother them; I wanted to face this with Barnabas. However, Barnabas reminded me that this is what friends and families are for.

Please do not place a burden in your heart because of me. God has made me strong, and together, we shall praise the Lord.

———————————

March 9, 1:20 a.m.

I write with my eyes closed. I am so tired.

Dear friends, in everything, give thanks to God!

I just got back after a long day with Margaret in the hospital. I left at 11:30 p.m. after Margaret fell asleep. Her spirit is high and without fear for the surgery that is going to take place in eleven hours.

Margaret and I continue to have faith in the Lord; we have no fear and worry. All we could think of and speak of is praise the Lord for His grace and mercy since we married. We have so many sweet memories as husband and wife, as father and mother, as friends and coworkers to many brothers and sisters in Hong Kong, the U.S., and China. We are so proud to have friends like you who are praying for us. We all believe that power comes from prayer. Let us use the privilege of prayer to ask our Lord to be in full control of our lives.

It is hard to imagine that we are relaxed because we have no fear. We did not ask the Lord just for healing. We asked the Lord that His will be done and to give us what is the best for us. If the cancer continues, we will face it with faith. It will be hard, but with God, nothing is impossible. After these five years working in China, we have learned so many great spiritual lessons. Now when the difficulty comes to us, it seems that our Lord has prepared us. Margaret and I have our hearts open to God and look at things in a different perspective. I trust you know me, that I am not saying anything to show off or to comfort you. When I say it, I mean it. We have peace of mind, and we have joy even in this crisis. I believe it could only come from our Lord, and how does it happen? It comes from your faithful prayers. Just in China, at least half a million underground Christians are praying for Margaret and for me. How can Satan win with such a strong prayer team? Two of my U.S. friends are fasting and praying these days until after the surgery on Wednesday, March 9, around 1:45 p.m. Many women in China conducted a prayer chain to pray 24 hours a day for ten days. My heart is just overwhelmed with love and thanksgiving. This is the sweetest moment in our lives even though it looks like a crisis. I knew in the very beginning that it is a blessing, and what a blessing!

When we checked into the hospital this morning, the nurses and doctors were so surprised with our attitude and with Margaret's laugh and smile. We explained to them that we have God. It seems that they do not understand exactly what we mean even though many of them are Christians, working at the Hong Kong Baptist Hospital.

Margaret will take the PET-CT scan today. I was told that this is the most advanced medical technology in the world to diagnosis cancer. Margaret drinks a special fluid and the doctor also injects it into her body. After an hour, he uses a special machine to scan the whole body to see if there are cancer tumors. The fluid will appear brightly on the screen if there are cancer tumors. We will learn the results two hours before the surgery. If the cancer has not spread to other parts of the body, then after the surgery, Margaret will be able to recover quickly. If not, Margaret will need to undergo further medical treatment.

This evening, we met with the three medical doctors who will conduct Margaret's surgery. The surgery is called radical hysterectomy (endometrial carcinoma). The good news is that this kind of cancer spreads slowly. Although Margaret's cancer is stage 2, it is controllable. If the cancer has not spread to other parts of the body, she has an 80 percent chance of recovery. We did not know these doctors; I just found one on the yellow pages and trusted the Lord. These three doctors have worked as a team for this kind of surgery for five years with 100 percent success. I am glad for our Lord's provision.

I have not told anyone in Hong Kong about Margaret except one of the camp staff. Since we have too many friends in Hong Kong, I do not want to draw too much attention. We cannot disclose to friends where we live for security concerns. In the Chinese culture, friends will visit you at your home if you are sick, and it is impolite to refuse their visit. However, we are not alone. We have you and so many friends in China who are praying.

Spiritual battles can only be fought with spiritual weapons. Other weapons do not work. Let us put our faith and prayer together to glorify our Lord.

Without fears and worry,

B

_____

March 9

Praise the Lord; EVERYTHING went well for Margaret.

Thank you for your prayers.

Today is a big day in our marriage because we have faced a critical crisis in our lives. I am glad to say that the Lord helped us to go through this crisis because of your love, concern, and prayers.

The operation went well. I waited outside the operating room for four hours. It was a serious surgery, but praise the Lord that everything went well. I had no fear and worry when I was waiting. No one was with me, and I do not need anyone. I have God, Jesus, and the Holy Spirit. I feel so close to the Lord because I understand that I have no other solution. The doctors can help with the medical treatment and operation, but the Lord controls the result.

Miracle—despite the fact that this kind of cancer spreads relatively slowly, the operation is a miracle because the affected area was huge. The tumor was large, but the cancer did not infect other organs and the damage to the body is little. The cancer was actually at stage 2, but the infected areas were at stage 1. After the surgery today, the cancer will be gone if the lab report is clear. We know, of course, the miracle is because of your prayers. Your prayers have given Margaret another life and given Margaret back to me because I might have lost her.

I praise the Lord for He controls my feelings. Fear, worry, depression, and anger toward God are very hard to control. I can keep myself close to the Lord, and I know there is only one way—my prayers and your prayers. This is the key for the growth of the House Church in China even though they are still under great persecution today. I have had joy in my heart during these eight days because I know and trust that God takes care of us, just as He cares for the underground Christians and pastors when they suffer for their faith.

When Margaret came out from the operating room, the first thing she asked me to do is to give thanks to the Lord. She could not speak, but she used her hand to signal that she wanted me to pray. We both had tears in our eyes because the Lord is great and faithful to all of us. He answers our prayers. Three hours later, when Margaret could speak, I asked her if she was afraid in the operating room. She said, "Of course not. Knowing that so many Christians in the East and in the West are praying, there is no reason to fear." The only feeling, the only feeling she had was that our friends and the Lord love her. That is the sweetest feeling that money cannot buy. We are just overwhelmed with joy. Again, what a blessing!

Eight full days have passed, and the crisis is almost over. Praise the Lord that He is in control and that He healed Margaret. The result could not be better. Please continue to pray for Margaret for her recovery—less pain and no infection.

Today is just like a normal day with the Lord's blessing! Everything that went well today comes from your prayer, and although I have said it too many times, I once again thank you for making the miracle happen and the crisis stop within a short period of time.

I will continue to update you on Margaret in the next few days. I sleep very well every night, and I know tonight will be even better.

———————

March 10

The Game is over—we win—because we pray. Margaret recovers well today.

I left the hospital last night at 10 p.m. and returned at

7:30a.m. Margaret slept well, and the doctor allowed her to have some water and congee (Chinese rice porridge). At around noon, she ate some crackers and started to exercise her hands and legs. She still has to stay in bed. In the late afternoon, the oxygen tubes and water injection bags were removed. The doctor said that Margaret is recovering very well, and she has never had any of her patients recover that well before. Praise the Lord. Prayer turns things around.

I bring in my computer and work beside her bed. During the day, we pray and talk, and she gets some good sleep. It is like our honeymoon . . . well, we love each other deeply. We are so thankful to the Lord that we are still together and committed to the ministry until we are in heaven.

In the evening, the doctors called to congratulate us because the lab result was much better than they expected. The cancer has not spread to other parts of the body, especially in the area close to the organ, which was taken out yesterday in the surgery. The cancer is 99.9 percent contained after the operation. It means the game is over. No more cancer, no more treatment, no chemotherapy is needed. Margaret just needs to have a checkup every three months for the next two years.

———————

March 13

Margaret has started to eat solid food like rice, some meat, and vegetables. She also has started to stand and walk a little bit. Everything is fine with her. The Lord is very kind to us, and He loves Margaret. We rejoice today for our Lord's guidance and His protection in our lives.

We shared the gospel with her roommate today, and we prayed with her and asked the Lord to heal her. Others in the ward have similar cases to Margaret.

The most precious lesson we have learned is how to

conquer fear, worry, and anxiety—pray and trust the Lord totally, ask for God's will to be fulfilled instead of just asking for healing. If I love Him, I will ask Him to just do whatever He wants to do to please Him—that is our attitude.

No fear, no worry, and no anxiety are great weapons to fight our enemy, Satan. I have learned this from the great examples of house church pastors and spiritual partners in China when they face persecution. We should fear God but no one and nothing else.

March 16

Margaret was released from the hospital today. We went home in early afternoon and Margaret has to adjust again to the bed, but it is good to be home (in Hong Kong). I am doing all the shopping and cooking, but I am happy to do it. I am very tired of staying at the hospital from 7:30 a.m. to 9:30 p.m., and now it is much easier to work at home instead of working on my computer at the hospital, which had no desk.

March 17–18

Praise the Lord always!

Margaret has to lie down in bed most of the time, but she is getting better and better. Margaret still cannot laugh loudly, but she can smile.

Our sons called several times in the last ten days to talk to Margaret, and she enjoys talking to them.

We have been so blessed in the past, but we have also prepared ourselves for personal and family crisis, such as having serious medical problem like cancer. Failure to prepare is preparing to fail. The most important issue for us is to give thanks to the Lord always. Even when we are in trouble, we trust our Lord loves us in all times and all circumstances.

Another thing we know is that the shortest distance between a problem and a solution is relatively equal to the distance between your knees and the floor. We pray and ask others to pray for us. We will accept the solution from the Lord, even if the cancer stays in the body.

Many people have the same cancer problem. We were so blessed to have so many Christians around the world praying for us: Vietnam, U.S., Taiwan, Canada, Mainland China, etc. We are so thankful to the Lord and to all of you. We cannot ask for more.

Thank you to you all!

As Margaret recovered in Hong Kong from the operation to remove her cancer, I stopped traveling into China for two months in early 2005. It was a difficult time, but God took care of us spiritually, physically, and financially.

My first trip back was to central China, where I would teach at an underground training center for four days. I stayed at a hotel my first night there, and woke the next morning to go to the training center where I would stay while I was teaching. When I walked out of the hotel, three ladies came to pick me up. We had to walk across the road and then to a van three blocks away to make sure we didn't attract any attention or were not being followed by the police.

While I crossed the road, two of the ladies surprised me by grabbing each of my wrists tightly. I told them, "Please do not do this! If someone took a picture of me with you two so close to me, people may think you are my wives in China and that will be the end of my ministry." Then didn't listen to me, so I had to forcefully pull away. I think they understood my concern, but they said, "Teacher An, we just respect you so much, so we want to take good care of you."

After crossing the street, one of the ladies gave me an envelope and said, "Teacher An, inside is 3,000 RMB, a personal donation from many brothers and sisters who have heard your teaching before. We know your wife just had an operation, so you probably need some money to cover the expenses."

I was so touched by their love. This is the love that I have experienced and seen all the time in China. Brothers and sisters who have little, some of them very poor, yet are willing to give everything they have to help someone else in need.

They also show great respect to pastors and teachers. At that time, there were few Bibles and no Bible study resources. They were so hungry for the Word of God, so truly excited to learn from someone who would come and teach them. They didn't take for granted what most in free countries do.

"No, I will not take your money," I told them. "God has been providing money for me to pay for the operation. Please use this money for the church ministry or for pastors who have greater needs than me."

God provided for Margaret and me. He provided her healing, and provided the funds to pay all the hospital expenses. It gave me great joy to give that money back to the church and to others, to show my thankfulness to God.

14

ONE-WAY TICKETS

Many years ago, I was flying from Chicago to Hong Kong. The person sitting next to me tried to talk to me. At first, I was tired and wanted to rest. I'm also not talkative and not inclined to make small talk with strangers. But the guy politely introduced himself and said he wanted to make new friends. It was a sixteen-hour flight, and I knew it would be hard to avoid talking to him for the entire time. It would also not be good if he found out I was a pastor and thought I was rude. After I had thought about these things, I said hi to him. But I had to be careful because of my work with the House Church in China. I couldn't tell him what kind of work I was really doing.

> "Hi, my name is Barnabas. I am from Hong Kong. Where are you from?"

> "My name is Gary Cheung, and I am also from Hong Kong. We can speak in Cantonese. I'm a screenplay writer and director for Radio Hong Kong. I like to talk to people to get ideas for my plays."

> "Great, I am a bit tired. I probably will take a nap soon after our flight takes off."

> "Yes, I am tired too, I will take a nap after lunch. Oh, what is your profession?"

I was still thinking how much I could tell him about myself, but at the same time, I thought this was a great opportunity to share the gospel, so I quietly prayed for wisdom.

> "I work for a large company."

Before I said my second sentence, Gary asked immediately:

"Oh, which company do you work for? A bank or big international company?"

"I work for a company that has branches in every country in this world!"

"Wow, what is the name of the company? Is your company on the U.S. or Hong Kong stock market?"

"No, we are a private company. We are not on the stock market."

"Who is the owner of your company? If you tell me the name of the owner or the chairman of the board, I may know the name of the company."

"The company is owned by a father and son and one more partner."

"Oh, a family business? I have never heard about a family business that has branches all over the world! Would you please tell me the name?"

I was able to open up the conversation from there and share with Gary about the Christian doctrine of the Trinity and Jesus Christ, our Savior.

Gary did not become a Christian after our talk, but he showed respect for my work as a pastor who served the House Church in China. He knew I was following the Lord Jesus Christ as my leader.

I didn't tell Gary the name of our HC Ministry, but I told Gary that Jesus is the CEO and CFO of my organization, and I'm like a COO—a manager accomplishing things under the leadership of my CEO. Before we landed in Hong Kong, as breakfast was served, Gary asked me, "Why do you call yourself a servant? You are actually the CEO of your operation. Why do you say that Jesus, this invisible "God," is your CEO and CFO? How does this work? You truly believe Jesus is God, and you can trust Him even when you have never met Him face-to-face?"

Again, I had another opportunity to share the love of Jesus with Gary. I told him my salvation story and told him that Jesus is love. I am just a servant of Jesus, no matter how people interpret my position in my organization.

We kept in contact for a few years and Gary finally became a Christian before he went to be with our Lord. He was older than I was and had cancer. I know he is in heaven now, and I will meet him again one day.

I began the HC Ministry in 2010 with my family and close supporters. My family moved back to Hong Kong to be closer to mainland China. We registered the ministry and set up the board of directors. By 2011, we were registered in the United States as well.

The HC Ministry was formed to serve the House Church in China. Our Chinese house church partners have always appreciated my friendship and our partnership. They love the Bible training we give them and the way we serve and love them. They are rarely, if ever, served in China, and it's special for them to receive that kind of love. It's important to me to keep promises, and whatever we say we'll do, we'll do it. We care deeply for them and listen to them, instead of telling them what we think they should do. Everything we do and coordinate, we do by word of mouth for security reasons. We never advertise, yet we serve so many house church pastors and churches. The HC Ministry is a small and unknown name in the world of Christian ministry. We are very different from the big names. We have only a small, dedicated staff to serve house church leaders, who in turn serve hundreds of thousands across China. We work with our house church partners in a functional and practical manner, in ways that truly help and serve the House Church rather than our own agenda.

A house church leader in China once asked me, "Why do you not do bigger things for the church in China? I know you are capable and reliable, and we like you!" I am not sure what he meant by "big." How do you define a big or small ministry? How does God define big and small? I know, for many people, "big" equals fame and notoriety.

Many years ago, I began to learn not to care about my own glory. I learned not to care who took the credit. This has helped me immensely in my work in China, where everything must be done in secret with no attention given to the church or myself. I have learned that humility is when someone is capable of doing something but doesn't have to show off. Humility is being willing to work behind the scenes.

Is it difficult or painful not to receive recognition for my hard work and ideas? No, because I've learned the greatest pain is not in suffering, but in disobedience and unrepentance to God. God wants us to give all the glory to Him. He invites us to work with Him and do it all for His glory.

In Chinese culture, it is important to bring honor to one's family and glory to one's ancestors. But even though I have been raised in that culture, I have a different perspective—a kingdom perspective that is greater than and supersedes not only my culture but all cultures. If my children do well in school, have a good job, make lots of money, and bring honor to me, where is God in that? He is not there because it's a form of disobedience. It denies God sovereignty over my children, who are *His* first and foremost.

I just want to care about God's servants one by one. I think that is big enough, to take care of God's people when they are in need. So I replied to the pastor, "Well, the problem is I am both a visionary and a doer, but I gave up my own vision a long time ago. I only have God's vision for His own kingdom. I work for Him, so I should not have my own vision. I am His servant, and He has asked me to serve the House Church in China."

Overall, the general misconception about house churches

is that individual house churches exist only in small, rural communities. In reality, house churches—and the networks to which they belong—exist in both rural and urban areas, in various forms and sizes, and meet in homes or other secret locations. Occasionally, rural house churches are larger and have their own simple building, usually a farmhouse. In urban areas, some house churches rent, own, or lease apartments or office space for meetings. Others meet in hotel conference rooms or restaurants each Sunday. There are house churches that are small, loosely formed, and family-based, as well as large-scale, highly organized churches with extensive networks. Some house churches are highly dependent upon Christian groups outside the country, while others are more self-sufficient. Some movements have official names, while others choose to remain nameless for security reasons.

I know it is hard for my friends and colleagues to understand how I trust my Lord. However, my family knows that when I say trust, it actually means I do not have the money for the project or the pastors that I promise to support. I say yes to them, not because I have a plan or know where to raise the money, nor because I have sympathy for them. I say yes because God has given me the wisdom and passion to say yes. I pray and ask my Lord Jesus, "If You were here, what would you do? Help or not help?" When I say yes, I trust my Lord, not myself, to provide for them. We do not take the credit. All glory goes to my Lord!

With the trust that is empowered to me by the Holy Spirit, I experience my Lord's provision for the house churches in China. As I experience His provision more and more, I have the courage to say yes, to promise to help, because I know God will approve the project, and He will help raise the funds for it.

I know many people, including my colleagues, think that I have connections to a lot of donors. They think I just email or call donors when I need money, but that is not true. I make only one phone call, a direct line with a number you all know.

I make a call to our friend Jesus for help.

As I said earlier, I have traveled to all the provinces and special regions of China except Tibet. I not only go to the cities to teach at urban churches and university student ministries, but I also travel extensively to many small towns and villages all over China, including the mountainous regions. I see the poverty in the villages that even many urban mainland Chinese could never imagine. However, it is exhilarating to see how these rural Christians sing and worship our Lord. It is also exciting to see how the rural pastors, who dress like farmers, some without socks and shoes, preach as someone with a PhD in theology. (Of course, many of them really are farmers and don't have money to dress nicely. Many pastors wear the same shirt every day for three or four months, until it is completely worn out, and then someone from the church buys them a new shirt). I truly believe if they ever have the opportunities I have had, they could exceed me and have a wonderful ministry in China.

I have met so many women who pray. Some even want to kiss me to show how much my support and love means to them, but I manage to avoid it every time. These women pray angelic prayers, which can last for an hour without any commas or repetition. Every word they say is very meaningful. I am from Hong Kong, where many pastors and Christians pray slowly. It is as though we are thinking about each word that we want to say. Our word count per minute is slow, but these Chinese women pray fast, not needing to stop for a breath. It is usually hard for Christians outside of China to spend more than one hour in a prayer meeting, but in the Chinese house churches, prayer is always for two to three hours. Many take turns to have overnight prayers on Friday night until Saturday morning, never repeating words or phrases, except "Amen!" and "Praise the Lord!"

Four years ago, I brought some Canadian friends to visit a village house church in central China. My guest asked the village pastor what time his Sunday service was. The pastor said, "It depends. Whenever the sun is rising, people start to walk to the church or meeting location, so the time is a little different each Sunday. It all depends on the first glimpse of the sun, and they wake up early to pray and watch the rising sun." It is truly amazing, and difficult for foreigners to understand the timing system in these villages. The villagers come to worship, sing, pray, study the Bible, and listen to preaching until noon. They spend more time than we do with our Lord, and I think what they do pleases Him. It's no surprise that the church in China is growing.

We are human beings, and we all have our weaknesses. The Chinese House Church Movement has its weaknesses. They can be influenced by bad Chinese culture, such as not upholding a contract or telling lies. Also, because everything is secret, it can sometimes be hard to discern the truth. But the church in China is growing under persecution. Why? We have to look at their spiritual strengths rather than their human weaknesses. We are all equal with our own human weaknesses, but the difference is that we lack the spiritual strength of the Chinese House Church. In addition to God's special blessing on them, they have many spiritual strengths, about which I am still learning. Spiritual strength has nothing to do with education, intelligence, money, strategy, planning, or our own power to achieve the goal we set for ourselves. It is about our hearts, how we love our Lord, and how much of ourselves we submit to Him!

Chinese house church Christians have submitted themselves to the Lord, and in doing so, they have developed their many strengths:

- The Way of the Cross is their glory. They take up their cross every day to follow Jesus.

- They are faithful and full of zeal to glorify God until their deaths. Their hearts are sold out for Jesus.

- They have implemented a radical migratory church planting strategy.

- They are never socially distant from God. They stay very close to God's heart. They pray, study the Bible, and want to experience God and to trust Him for their provision. They have seen and experienced the Lord's work during difficult times (John 20:18).

- They are always hungry for the Word of God.

- They know Jesus is building His church in China, which communism cannot destroy. Therefore, they are not afraid of persecution. They only ask for strength to face persecution and willingness to suffer for the gospel.

- They pray. When their life gets too hard to stand, they kneel and pray. The House Church of China knows how to pray.

- They don't just talk, they do. They are on fire for the gospel. In season and out of season, they go and evangelize.

- They reveal the DNA of Jesus Christ through embracing everything in love, overcoming evil with good, and walking in step with God.

The Chinese House Church Movement is a well-kept secret. When I spend time with them, I feel like I have discovered a treasure, and they are always teaching me important spiritual lessons.

The growth of the Chinese House Church Movement is indeed not shifted by the will of the party-state. There is no five-year plan, nor any pre-planned budget. The leaders do not have a conference every year to discuss church growth plans or strategies. Many leaders do not even know each other, because they are spread out across China and communication can be dangerous.

When I study the Bible and the life of Jesus, I see how He repeatedly changed His itinerary and disrupted His schedule. Many times, as He moved from one place to another to preach, He would stop to give attention to just one person in need. Almost all of these people were the underprivileged, with no one to care for them; but our Lord Jesus stopped, listened, talked, touched, healed, and freed them. He served with the needs of people on His heart and mind. The Chinese House Church movement serves like Jesus. They do not have a fixed church service schedule as we do when we worship. They will spend an extra thirty minutes to pray for just one person, and I have seen miracles happen because of their prayers. The House Church seems to be losing their battle with the government, but they are winning the spiritual battle because they trust our Lord.

Politics is full of calculations, but love cannot be calculated. The love of Jesus is unconditional and sacrificial. We all know what the result of the battle will be in the end. Jesus is the winner. We are on Jesus' side, as is the House Church in China. Therefore, we serve them in many different ways, each one designed to meet their needs, not what we believe their needs should be.

HOUSE CHURCH PASTORS

Guangming, whose name means "bright light," has been a fulltime pastor since the 1970s. As a child, he learned about Jesus from his Christian parents, who often held gatherings and services in their home.

He was called to be a pastor for the House Church and attended a six-month secret Bible training in the village. After the training, his church sent him to plant and pastor churches in villages he had never visited, and where there were no Christians. These villagers already had a concept of God and spirits, but they needed to know the truth. When they heard his message, many villagers gave up their superstitious beliefs and accepted the gospel.

Guangming has been chased by the police and arrested.

His churches have been shut down, and he has faced much persecution and opposition. He has lived in poverty and unstable conditions his entire life, yet he has remained faithful for decades.

Guangming's story is very common for many house church pastors. Their lives are never easy. Unstable finances, an unceasing workload, and constant travel deal a heavy blow to their family life. Tensions arise, and conflicts occur. In fact, during the early days of the house church revival, church planters were taught to heed Paul's advice and remain unmarried for the rest of their lives.

Rural pastors and urban pastors face entirely different challenges. When rural church planters and their families begin ministering in a new area, they must sometimes live in empty fields or caves. They ask God to lead them to a family they can convert and subsequently live with. Once in the care of their newly formed congregations, a pastor and his family are provided with food, clothing, and shelter. Cash, medicine, and other supplies, however, are difficult to obtain. These pastors are often responsible for leading five to six house churches in an area as large as sixty square miles. In impoverished regions, pastors must visit their congregations on foot. In more affluent areas, congregations may be able to purchase a bicycle or motorcycle for their leader.

Unlike their rural counterparts, urban pastors face a much higher cost of living, making financial stability a necessity.

House Church Planters

The Chinese House Church movement has implemented a radical migratory church planting strategy. This approach took shape in the early 1980s in central China, where the Yellow River was once the center of civilization of China. This includes the provinces of Henan and Anhui, which are population centers and home to some of the largest house church movements. There was a large wave of persecution in 1983, so the house churches started to send out "migrating church planters." These church planters would go two-by-two, with one-way train tickets and about 150 renminbi each (about twenty U.S. dollars), to an unreached area. They would begin evangelizing as soon as they stepped off the train. The first converts would often become host families, providing a place for the church to begin meeting, and for the church planters to stay.

In the early 2000s, two female church planters, about eighteen years old, were sent from their church to China's northernmost province, Heilongjiang. They had finished their Bible school training, and they were given about 150 renminbi each and one-way tickets to the small town of Suihua. They didn't have any connections there. They had no means to do research or a survey. They had looked at a map and picked a random town. They went out with joy. As they were taught in their Bible school about the Way of the Cross, so they were willing to bear their cross to follow Christ every day.

They arrived during the winter, and the town, situated between North Korea and Russia, was bitterly cold. They had no place to stay, but trusted the Lord to open a home for them. The first night, they slept at the train station, and spent the next day looking for people with whom to share the gospel. But it was so cold, and the town was buried in snow. No one was on the streets, so it was difficult for them to find anyone. They had very little money, so they ate as little as possible.

They slept in the train station the second night and went out the third day. After walking around, they became disoriented due to their unfamiliarity with the village, as well as everything being covered with snow. As night approached, they couldn't find their way back to the station. They had no cell phones or data. They had no one to help them. They were hungry and tired, and they collapsed in the snow, falling asleep in the sub-freezing temperature.

When the sun came up the next morning, one of the girls awoke to see dazzling white all around her. She thought she had died from hypothermia and all the white she saw was heaven. Then she realized she was still alive, and it had snowed even more during the night. She thought her friend has died, and was surprised when she was able to wake her up.

The girls were surprised that they felt warm, as though they had been covered during the night. As they stood up, they saw animal footprints in the snow next to them. Their clothes also had an animal smell on them. They realized that God had sent animals to lie on their bodies after they had fallen asleep to keep them alive. They prayed, thanking God and asking Him to provide food because they were so hungry.

A woman from the village approached them and invited them to her house, where she would give them food and let them warm up. They shared the gospel with her. She gave her life to Jesus, and the church began in her home.

Church planters, such as these two girls, have contributed significantly to the growth of the House Church in China over the past forty years. Church planters are on the road for years on end, so they have no home congregations to support them, and they receive minimal funding from their movements, who have little to spare. The HC Ministry supports these church planters at the front lines through a variety of means, including monthly support for up to three years, transportation expenses, and medical fees. I believe these church planters are vital to the growth of the House Church.

BIBLES AND BIBLE STUDY MATERIALS

I had finished preaching at a church in Zhengzhou when a new believer approached me. He thanked me for preaching and encouraging the people there. He told me he was a new believer in Christ who had been a communist for many years. He had witnessed to his family. His wife and twenty-year-old son had also become Christians, but they still did not have Bibles. He told me:

> *"Our pastor told us we are on the waiting list for a Bible. We have to wait for someone from outside China to donate a Bible for us, because we cannot buy Bibles in China. There are no Bibles for sale in any bookstores where I live. Barnabas, please help us. My family really wants to know Christ more and study the Bible. Please pray for us that our Lord will provide a Bible for my family."*

Imagine being on a waitlist to have a Bible. This is a great need of the House Church, one that we have worked hard to meet. There are groups that smuggle Bibles into China, but I have always thought it more efficient and cost-effective to print Bibles domestically through underground printing presses. Underground presses are typically owned and operated by faithful Christians who are willing to take on the danger, or they are run by non-believers who overlook the risks in order to earn extra money. So our HC Ministry pays for the printing of Bibles as well as the distribution costs.

Official Chinese government sources deny the notion of a Bible shortage in China, as do many Western mission organizations and Bible societies. In reality, House Church workers are desperate for millions of copies of God's Word for the masses of believers, especially for those in the outlying areas, who have little hope of ever acquiring a Bible.

Today, thanks to the help of many generous Christians from outside China, many pastors and Bible school students in urban areas have their own copy of Scripture. However, for average believers in the countryside, Bibles remain difficult to obtain. Many Christians share copies of God's Word among themselves, and continue to memorize the Scriptures as a practical means of coping with the shortage. In some outlying areas, Bibles are still being copied by hand and shared between many people. As many as twenty million believers do not have a physical Bible, and as the church continues to grow exponentially, the need becomes even more acute. Thanks to technological advancements, thumb drives (USBs) containing entire Bibles and theological courses are becoming more common. We distribute these in areas of China where it's too difficult or dangerous to have a physical Bible. The contents of the drives are easily copied and shared between believers.

Mary* is a forty-year-old primary school teacher who lives and works in the rural mountains of Hubei Province. A local house church pastor shared the gospel with her for a long time, and she finally came to Christ after she was healed from an illness in early 2020. She wanted to share the Bible with her students at school. Because of her remote location, there is more autonomy and freedom to do so without too much interference from local officials. However, she has no access to Bibles because there are hardly any bookstores in rural areas, not to mention government-approved Three-Self church bookstores that are authorized to sell Bibles. (Even if you can get to a Three-Self bookstore, you will still be questioned about your identity and reasons for obtaining a Bible. They will ask, "If you are not a member of the Three-Self, why do you need to obtain a Bible?"). Mary's story is common throughout China, and underscores the need to continue to put Bibles into the hands of believers.

BIBLE SCHOOLS

Feng was born in rural northern Henan Province in the 1970s. When he was a boy, a church planter came to his village to host an evangelistic meeting. He attended with his family, and they all accepted the gospel. Their lives were renewed and utterly changed.

Feng and his entire family fully committed themselves to serve the Lord in a variety of ways, the most significant of which was hosting a house church in their home. Due to persecution, house churches and Bible trainings were forced underground, figuratively and often literally. Feng's family dug out a basement specifically to be used as a Bible school, and accepted young candidates from all over China to attend. Feng's family hosted the students in their home, and also took care of security and surveillance outside the home.

Sadly, in April of 1988, the police discovered what they were doing and raided their home. The police not only confiscated every item of value (which was typical of police raids at the time and is common again today), including furniture, kitchenware, and personal valuables, but also all Bibles and other literature. Feng's father was also arrested and spent a year in prison. After enduring much physical hardship in prison, the police released him, but he died soon after. Feng, who has since become a pastor, has also been arrested many times throughout his ministry. He was once detained in jail for forty days, interrogated every day, beat by police batons, and endured many physical and spiritual hardships.

Even so, Pastor Feng and his family remained undeterred in their spirit and service, as the Apostle Paul said in Romans 8:35: "Who shall separate us from the love of Christ? Shall trouble or hardship or persecution or famine or nakedness or danger or sword?"

These underground Bible schools are vital for preparing church planters and pastors. Many of these schools are operated by a single movement, and have limited connections outside China. However, for the schools that we support, we provide dedicated instructors and training materials from around the world. We also work to unify the house churches, by welcoming students from all the different movements to our Bible schools. Together, these devoted believers study the Bible and grow spiritually.

Small, secret Bible schools concealed across China are packed with committed Christians, sometimes as young as fourteen years old. They fervently hide God's Word in their hearts and prepare to be the next generation of fearless house church leaders. These young people's thorough preparation carries them through their lives and ministries, no matter what they encounter. Whether they face arrests, beatings, imprisonment, or death, their time of preparation in prayer, study, and memorization provides them with a solid and sure foundation for walking in the "Way of the Cross."

SUPPORT FOR PASTORS IMPRISONED FOR THEIR FAITH

Lily* is a church planter who works alongside her husband James*. However, in March 2019, James was imprisoned for the gospel and has still not been released. Since then, Lily has led their church. It is not an easy task. The police harass Lily every week, threatening that if she does not close the church, they will put her in prison as well. Lily and James have an eight-year-old son, so Lily is concerned for him and does not want to be arrested. However, she cannot do what the government tells her to do—to remove the cross at her church, hang the current president's photo and communist slogans in its place, and to attend a re-education camp.

In China, a pastor's imprisonment is preceded by a sequence of events. First, a pastor is charged with wrongdoing. He may be accused of disturbing social order, illegally sharing the gospel, or participating in anti-revolutionary activities, depending on the activity for which he was arrested. Regardless of the charge, he will not receive a trial.

In some regions, authorities interrogate the pastors non-stop for hours—sometimes days—attempting to learn how the house church movements are run, how many believers attend, where the meeting places are, and who is in charge. Multiple officers take rotating shifts to interrogate the prisoner. Following the example of Jesus before the Sanhedrin (Mark 14:60–61), the pastors do not answer questions. They are then punished for their silence.

Until the beginning of 2014, pastors were placed in labor camps—essentially factories that produced commercial goods with "free" labor. Inmates were required to work long days, often 18-hour shifts, to meet a specified quota, only to have their quota gradually increased to impossible levels. When the prisoner failed to produce his assigned share, he was punished, often with a beating. With each subsequent failure, the prisoner endured more beatings. While the Chinese government announced early in 2014 that all labor camps would be closed, the punishment of imprisoned believers continues. This may be the same form of persecution, but referred to by a different name, or may be another type of persecution altogether.

In the government's attempt to control the underground church and break its leaders of their commitment to Christ, they watch these pastors, threaten them, and make their lives miserable in hopes that they will give up on ministry.

Cal* came to Christ at eighteen years old. He and his wife have faithfully served the Lord for more than thirty years and now serve as theological trainers for their movement. They developed their own two-year curriculum, and each class hosts about fifteen students.

Cal's home also serves as a small meeting place. One time, he hosted a traveling church planter from another province, and before the service had ended, the police surrounded and raided his home. They arrested him, his uncle, and four other leaders at his church. Cal was detained at the local jail for one-and-a-half months. Cal was beaten, and another pastor's legs were beaten until they bled and swelled. His family was denied visiting rights, and the police only allowed their loved ones to pass some clothing to them. For Cal, the most painful part was not being allowed to read Scripture, pray, or worship. If they discovered him doing any of these things, he was beaten.

However, some sisters from the church sewed small copies of Bibles into the quilts that the police allowed them to send. Therefore, Cal and the other pastors would cautiously read Scripture whenever they could. Many believers from Cal's church also sang hymns and worshiped loudly on the hill across from the jail, which greatly comforted him and his fellow pastors. Cal was a farmer, and it was harvest season during his imprisonment. The believers from his church helped his wife with the harvest, and they were able to harvest all the crops without any loss.

When a pastor like Cal is imprisoned, his family's situation depends largely on why he was arrested. Repercussions are much more serious if the local authorities interpret the pastor's "crime" as severe. In some cases, the pastor's home may be raided and all family possessions confiscated. The position and function of the pastor's wife also plays a role. If the wife is a pastor herself, or is directly involved in church leadership (which is often the case), she may be vulnerable to arrest, interrogation, and in extreme cases, imprisonment. If she is a housewife or holds a job outside the home and church, the authorities keep a close watch on her activity.

A pastor's wife, therefore, knows she must maintain a low profile after her husband's arrest. She must avoid contact with other Christians and pastors. She must not attend house church meetings because she can never be certain if she is under surveillance by the authorities. In most cases, she shoulders this tremendous burden alone, relying entirely on God's provision and protection. On occasion, members of the congregation may covertly bring her and her children food and financial support. There is, of course, a range of what, and how much, is given to imprisoned pastors' families within China's millions of house churches. In addition to offerings from individuals and local house churches, the larger house church movements may also have modest emergency funds in place for these situations.

TRAINING & SEMINARS

When I began the HC Ministry, I asked John Bechtel many times to serve on our board. However, he had worked hard for many years and was ready to retire. But he kept his interest to know and understand what I was doing in China for the house church movements.

Then, in April of 2008, John was on a work trip in a different country in Asia. He knew many pastors there, and he started to think it would be a good idea to build a training center outside of China. John had traveled to China with me to visit house churches after his retirement, and he understood that it was increasingly difficult to train large groups of pastors in China. At the time, it was possible to train them in Hong Kong, but facilities that were sufficient to host large groups were expensive, and drew attention from government officials, both in China and Hong Kong.

After the 2008 Beijing Olympics, many people thought China would be more open. But in reality, many of our trainings had been canceled due to police intervention, even when teachers and pastors had already arrived at the site. A lot of money was being wasted, and we had no way to avoid it. So building a training center outside of China would cost money, but in the long run, we would save money. Large groups leaving China wouldn't draw attention, and housing them in this country with our own facilities would be cost-effective.

John's work in the past had allowed him to make connections in this country. If the funds could be raised, he was confident he could find the right people to build and operate it. I agreed and prayed the project would be funded. Our fundraising was met with immediate excitement, and donors began promising funds. The project moved ahead quickly, and land was purchased and the center was built. In March 2013, the HC Ministry began to use the facility. During the first year, we conducted four seminars. Since then, we've held eight to nine seminars every year. The HC Ministry began officially operating the center in May 2015, and we took on all the financial responsibilities at the same time. In 2017, we doubled our training capacity from sixty pastors to 120 with the construction of a new three-story dorm building.

Each seminar provides house church pastors with an amazing experience. They receive solid biblical instruction on a variety of topics including theology, sermon preparation, Bible interpretation, evangelism, and worship. They also enjoy times of fellowship, praise, prayer, and rest.

Over the years, I have witnessed many foreign organizations work in China and try to help the House Church. Oftentimes, however, they only cause more problems for the church. One particular ministry wanted to help house church pastors by giving them six-month trainings in countries such as United States, Korea, and Singapore. This ministry is also charismatic and tends to make decisions quickly, with little concern for the practical and spiritual outcomes.

These house church pastors were already serving their local congregations as well as running local seminaries. Abruptly offering pastors the opportunity to study abroad for six months is like dangling a carrot in front of their faces. Of course, they would want to go abroad. However, the resulting consequences aren't considered: Many of them come from impoverished backgrounds, and if a better life can be obtained, particularly for their children, they would do whatever they can to make it happen.

One of the locations for the six-month training was in the United States. Most Chinese, if given the opportunity, would find a way to stay behind and never return to China or their churches, regardless of immigration laws. In fact, some of the house church pastors who did eventually stay abroad later admitted to me that they were very miserable. They didn't know the language and never realized how difficult it would be to adjust to a different culture. Although they want to stay abroad for their children's education, they feel guilty since they may not be able to serve the Lord as effectively as when they were in China. Whenever our HC Ministry takes any house church pastors abroad, we graciously yet firmly ensure their faith is strong and their calling to serve the House Church *in*

China is affirmed. We make sure that the trip is not particularly long and that their visit abroad is a temporary one. They are expected to return home. This is a sensitive issue that needs to be handled carefully and sensibly. The opportunity to travel abroad, especially five to ten years ago, is too great a temptation for those who may not be ready for it.

Other ministries fundraise and spend a lot of money to host global conferences. I have worked with many big names from big mission agencies to organize large training seminars and conferences. They ask me for connections with the house church movements, but they ditch me immediately after they get what they want. I know and expect it will happen, but I still do it because I do not believe my partners in China are mine to own. God can benefit my house church friends through these agencies. But many times, these agencies are all talk and no action. They say, "We are visionaries with visions." The word "vision" sounds great, but is it really from the Lord? How much of donors' money has been wasted when ultimately nothing is done? Many churches and ministries have asked us for help to recruit connections for *their* vision tours and trainings. They promise us money for our time and expenses, but ultimately they never pay, and still owe us money to this day.

Some organizations spend a lot of money on books, music, or study guides to distribute in China, but the message is neither profound nor culturally relevant, and therefore has no lasting power. To be honest, I wonder, what is their ultimate purpose? Is it to break into the Chinese Christian market with their materials? Are they wealthy people who want to do something significant by throwing a lot of money at a project, without the necessary research and respect for their target audience?

Our HC Ministry does not focus on fundraising, but God has given us partners that help us raise funds for our ministry in China. Most university or NGO presidents spend at least 75 percent of their time fundraising, even though they have development officers or fundraising departments. We have a ministry budget that's approved by our board every year, but there are projects and needs in the field that are not in the budget. By faith, we do them anyway. God provides the funds later. His provision is sufficient.

People think I am crazy, but all my life, God has been providing. From 2009 to 2011, I went through difficult times after I left my previous ministry and started the HC Ministry. However, God has carried us through the valley of deep shadows, prepared a table for me in front of my enemies, poured oil on my head, and given me an overflowing cup.

Often, the leaders of Christian NGOs only meet people to raise money. They don't really care about the people themselves; they only care about their pockets. God will not bless this type of meeting. We should care about people, and when they are blessed by our visit, they will give to God.

I graduated from college with a double major in business administration and political science, and a minor in economics. I like to look at world politics through an economic eye. However, I believe that in the divine economy, there is no recession or financial turmoil. There is only grace.

I am not a financial planner. I do not invest in stock, simply because I don't have the money or the time to spend on the stock market. I believe we will not have negative equity in kingdom work. Bankruptcy means we are unable to pay our outstanding debts. In kingdom work, we will never be in bankruptcy, because God owns everything. But we have to be careful that we are not in spiritual bankruptcy. I pray every day for myself. If I am not following my Lord and His Way of the Cross, I will stop and pick up my cross.

The Lord's Prayer says He gives us our daily bread, not that He gives us bread for the whole month. He wants us to trust Him daily, which I am still learning. We have to empty ourselves. Otherwise, there is no room for God's grace.

I was often dismissed as a "doer" and not a visionary. I was thought of as only being capable to carry out the visions of other visionaries. I find that to be untrue. The Lord has shown me what needs to be done, and He has provided me the tools to do it. I find it repulsive for those who are all talk, and raise and spend lots of money with nothing to show for it, to steal from God and His people.

My life goal is to be a faithful servant of my Lord. That will determine my success. Success is peace of mind in knowing I did my best. I always prepare myself. I have walked 15,000 steps a day since the summer of 2014 to prepare myself physically. Failure to prepare is preparing to fail. God trained me hard both when I was a boy, and after I became a Christian, in order to change my character. He taught me to be more concerned with my character than with my reputation. My character is who I really am, while my reputation is merely what others think of me. "Ability may take you to the top, but it takes character to keep you there." That quote is from John Wooden, the American head basketball coach of UCLA. He coached UCLA to ten NCAA national championships in a twelve-year period, including a record seven in a row.

I am a firm believer that I am just a servant. I am not the leader of the ministry. "Deacon" in the Bible means servant, not leader. I believe as a servant, in my work and service, I need to use my heart more than my brain, because my intelligence will never compare to God, who is my boss.

The Bible also says that Jesus will build His church, so nothing I want to build is mine. I am just doing the work Jesus wants me to do. I am a servant. Jesus offered a three-year servant-leadership course to His twelve disciples, but it seems they did not really understand Jesus' teaching until he died for our sins on the cross. After Jesus' resurrection, the disciples went out to spread the good news of Jesus Christ and plant churches, and more and more people became Christians.

Jesus led by example. For Jesus, there was only one plan and ultimate purpose for Him to come to this earth. He did not come by a private jet. He was born in a humble manner in a small town called Bethlehem. His plan was to go to Calvary and die on the cross. Jesus led with the heart of a servant. He served with the heart of a king.

Most Bible scholars believe His disciples were all executed for the gospel, except John. He was persecuted and exiled to the island of Patmos, where he wrote the last book of the New Testament, The Revelation.

Jesus is the greatest leader, because He led by example. We serve Him not to be rich, but because we are inspired by Him. He conquered the world not by armed force, but by His love. Jesus' ministry was not based on numbers, but on His sacrificial love. Love does not necessarily cost money; it costs time and heart. Jesus spent thirty-three years on this earth. His love saved me and made me humble.

What can I offer to the King of Kings? Nothing but my life. I am willing to be His servant my whole life long. I am blessed to have Jesus as my leader and Lord. I have spent half of my life causing problems, and the other half solving them. I made mistakes and got myself into fights. Now, I let God fight my battles instead of fighting the battle myself. I learned to understand the extent of His love every day. Jesus monitors my spiritual, emotional, and mental health so that I will not hurt others, and if I feel I am being hurt, Jesus can heal my broken heart.

As a servant of God, I am serving my Lord happily — with less ego and more love and respect for others.

———————————

If there is rain, all the raindrops are blessings from the Lord.

If there is wind, then all the greetings in the air are God's greetings.

If there is sunshine, the warmth that shines on you is God's care and love.

———————————

15

SLEEPING IN THE MIDDLE

China, 2003

"No, dear brother, I cannot," I insisted.

I didn't want to offend by saying no any more firmly, but what else could I say as this sincere Christian family insisted I share their bed with them?

It was the middle of December in northeast China along the border of Russia and North Korea. The weather was incredibly cold. I had just finished teaching in the tiny, poor village for five hours to a group that didn't even have enough chairs to sit on. Many sat on the freezing ground with only newspapers for a cushion.

After my teaching, I was led to a small village home, fewer than one hundred square feet in size. I walked inside to a single room with a large stove and only one bed. It was warm, but I thought, "Where are the other beds? Where will I sleep?"

I think the husband could see the look on my face. He told me:

"Dear teacher, you're our honored guest in this house. We haven't hosted anyone in our home before, so tonight is very special! You're a great teacher, and since we have only one big bed, you will be sleeping in the middle of it. I will sleep on your right side, my wife will sleep on your left side, my ten-year-old son will sleep beside me, and my twelve-year-old daughter will sleep beside my wife. I think this is a perfect arrangement. Let me get you some water to wash your face, your hands, and your feet."

"Wow," I thought. "I can't do this! This is too weird for me to sleep between this husband and his wife." However, they were sincere believers, and their motivation was their Christ-like love for the church and me. What could I do? I told him I couldn't:

> *"I'm not used to sleeping next to someone who isn't my wife. I can sleep on the floor, or if there is a motel nearby, I can pay to stay there."*

> *"No, no, no, dear teacher!"* he pleaded with me. *"It will be an honor to me and my wife for you to sleep between us. You will bring a great blessing to my church and my family. Please stay! Besides, this is a small, poor village with no motel."*

We went back and forth for a few minutes. I offered to sleep on the floor next to the stove, or even on the side of the bed. But every protest was met with insistence I allow them to honor me in this way. How could I say no?

During my time in ministry, I've experienced the love and sacrifice of believers in many different ways. Many times, I'm overwhelmed by their hospitality and generosity. Other times, it comes in unexpected ways that I've learned to accept as love, even if it's foreign to me.

So that night, I lay in the big bed in their tiny home, between this dear brother, his wife and their children—and didn't dare fall asleep! I kept both arms under my back, afraid that if I fell into a deep sleep or had a dream, I may not remember where I am, and kiss the woman next to me thinking she's my wife, Margaret!

But what a wonderful experience! They showed me love through their actions, even though it was in a way that was difficult for me to appreciate at the time. Since then, I have tried to understand how different people express love, so that I can show love to each person in a way they can accept!

Many commencement speakers like to tell graduating college students, "Are you ready? Go change the world! The world is yours!" It's a good slogan but hardly true. Only a few people can really change the world. In my graduation speech to our Bible seminary students, I always tell them, "Do not think you can change the world. Only God has that power. Trust God to give you the power not to be changed by the world! I believe the Holy Spirit is our agent of change!" I usually continue to say, "If after ten years, you have not been changed by the world, are still on fire for the gospel, and are still serving God as a pastor, then you are a successful man or woman."

Change can be good or bad. Oftentimes, we do not like change because it makes us break out of our comfort zone. When I leave my comfort zone and really trust and follow God, miracles happen. That is when I experience God working in me and my life.

Creating change and moving outside your comfort zone might mean sleeping between a sincere husband and wife, who show you love in a way you can't comprehend. It might mean using the bathroom while a Christian earnestly asks you questions, or wants to ensure you're safe outside at the toilet late at night.

———————————

In January of 2014, I was invited to speak to house church leaders at a retreat in China. Over 300 pastors and church planters attended the three-day conference. The conference was held in a big barn house, which had been converted into a church. Local officials in the province knew these pastors, and some of them were even secret believers. So they protected the church, but they could not attend themselves, because they were afraid the higher authorities would find out about the meeting and punish them.

Pastors of this movement came from all over China. I taught for three sessions and met with many groups. We had many great discussions about Christianity in China, and how they can respond to persecution.

Unfortunately, the toilet situation in the village was not modern, even in 2014. There were no partitions, no flushing water, and no toilet bowls—only a row of holes in the ground next to each other. You could do your business and talk to your neighbor at the same time. I was only going to be there one night, so I thought I could deal with it.

The teaching and meetings were finished at 11 p.m., and then the host brought me to his home to stay for the night. The father, who was still young, said he was building a new, modern toilet, and had wanted to finish it before I arrived. But he couldn't get the right parts from the shop, so it was unfinished. I told him it was fine and it was only for one night. We talked for almost forty-five minutes before I could get ready to bed. After brushing my teeth and washing my face, all of a sudden, the need to use the toilet hit me. I wanted to wait until the next evening after I returned to the hotel in the city, but I knew I couldn't. I asked the host:

> *"Hi Brother Lee, if I need to go number two, where should I go?"*

> *"Teacher An, no problem. My toilet is not ready for you. I'm sorry, but there's a public toilet nearby, and I can take you there."*

> *"Good, I do need to go. Sorry to bother you this late!"*

> *"No problem, Teacher An. The movement asked me to take good care of you. Let me find my big flashlight because there's no electricity or lights inside the toilet."*

> *"I will bring my flashlight too, so I should be fine."*

We walked for about five minutes. To my surprise, the toilet had walls, but it still was only holes in the ground and very smelly.

My host was right next to me, so I told him:

"Brother Lee, you can go home. No need to wait for me. I remember how I got here, and it's easy to go back since it's a straight walk and just one turn. Thank you so much!"

"No, no, no, Teacher An! I'm here to serve you! I will wait here while you use the toilet."

I knew I couldn't argue with him or convince him otherwise, so I walked to the toilet where, at 12:15 a.m., at least nine people were squatting in the dark next to each other. Suddenly, a loud voice cried out behind me, "Praise our Lord! He has prepared a place for you even in a public toilet." It was my eager host, Brother Lee, coming to check on me.

The only empty spot was right in the middle. I began to take care of my business when the light of Brother Lee's flashlight blinded me. He was standing in front of me, completely illuminating all of me.

"Brother Lee, please wait outside! I am fine here."

"No, no, no, I need to take care of you. It is so dark here! I will stand here and have the light shine on you."

"Dear Brother Lee, please wait outside. I am not used to this. I have my flashlight on, and I will be fine!"

I could hear the other nine men around me all laughing—a "foreigner" coming to use a Chinese village toilet.

"No, Teacher An, it is my responsibility. We love you so much, and we need to protect you. You are our honored guest. Since you are not used to this kind of toilet, I will be here to serve you."

"Thank you for your kindness!"

I knew I could not argue or convince him otherwise. So I gave up and continued with my business. Then we walked back to the house together.

They loved me very much, but they expressed their love in a way that was difficult for me to appreciate. Still, I tried to allow them to love me in their way, because I knew how much it meant to them.

God has taught me that to serve means letting go of my dignity and preferences. To serve means to accept the love given to me, even if it is difficult for me to accept. I also need to love others with the love they need and will accept.

———————————

That is how we must love the House Church in China. We must love and serve them even if it is unfamiliar and uncomfortable for us. They don't need foreign organizations telling them what they need. They don't need well-intentioned foreigners rejecting their acts of love. They need Christians with a willing heart who are called by God to serve their fellow brothers and sisters in China.

The church in China needs the partnership of the West, but too often, Western Christians who visit China for the first time expect to be ministering to the Chinese believers. Instead, they leave feeling that they have been ministered to. We can learn much from the strong, enduring faith of our brothers and sisters in China.

The spiritual soil of Communist China consists of both fertile and stony ground. Those lacking a genuine encounter with Christ soon turn their backs on the church, because they are unable to withstand the persecution. But when God nurtures His seeds of truth, He develops strong and fervent believers who flourish spiritually in spite of—and perhaps because of—the terrible persecution they endure. Christians in China possess a genuine faith. They are not Sunday Christians; rather, they are daily Christians who carry their faith into all of life's circumstances. As you read this, many are languishing in jail for their faith. Others quickly pick up where those arrested left off. They continue to teach and preach to the ends of China and beyond — knowing they may soon face the same consequences.

When partnering with the church in China, you will be humbled. You will be brought to tears when you hear stories of faith, persecution, and endurance that most Westerners have never come close to facing. You will experience their genuine humbleness and spiritual wisdom that doesn't come through reading commentaries or books about how to live great lives. Instead, it is learned through fiery trials, during which they throw themselves at the feet of God, who pours out His loving-kindness and sustains them miraculously through it all.

———————————

It was May 2006. I had been on the bus in central China for hours. I had left a major city, and was only two stops away from my final destination, where I would speak to a group of pastors and Bible students. Suddenly, one of my cell phones rang. I knew that could be a bad sign. An urgent voice asked me:

"Are you Teacher An?"

"Yes," I replied, and then cautiously asked, *"What is the color today?"*

"Yellow and red."

I was relieved. He had answered our code phrase correctly. We each knew the other wasn't a spy.

"Great, you are my brother. What's happening?"

"Dear teacher, please do not come. The weather here is so bad we cannot entertain you."

The phone went dead. I knew what he meant by "weather." He was talking about the police, and they must have been out in force. So I got off the bus at the next stop and took another bus back to the city. I didn't know what was happening, but I was praying for my brothers and sisters.

That morning, the pastor who ran the Bible school had received a call from his nephew, who worked at the police station. Although the nephew wasn't a Christian, he called his uncle, telling him the weather wasn't good. The police were coming to shut down his Bible school. The pastors and students waiting for me had to flee. They were used to receiving calls and running quickly before the police arrived, so within five minutes of the call, they had hidden all the Bibles in an underground compartment and covered all signs of the school.

As three police cars sped to the school to arrest the teachers and students, a huge sandstorm roared in, so thick that the police cars had to stop because they couldn't see where they were driving.

The storm raged for twenty minutes. When the storm finally relented, every house was covered in sand and looked the same. The police officers had no way to discover which house served as the Bible school from the description they were given. They drove around the village for thirty minutes before giving up and returning to the station.

When they got back to the station, the nephew overheard them talking about their failed mission:

> *"It was a waste of time! We're so unlucky. We thought we'd find this underground Christian training center, destroy it, and arrest all the Christians and pastors. What a huge sand storm! The sand even covered all the footprints on the dirt road that may have given us clues to find them. What a disappointing day!"*

Their disappointment was our excitement! We know our Lord answers our prayers. He protects his servants.

God is seeking those who are willing to partner with and serve the House Church in China. I am what I call a "small potato"—a man who was born a poor orphan, was saved by God, and is now used as God sees fit. I am overjoyed to serve my brothers and sisters, who show me what faith is every day.

I am glad to share their burdens as their brother in Christ. God gives me wisdom when I need to teach, knowledge when I need to preach, and strength when I need to run, even when I'm barefoot. Hudson Taylor said, "Doing God's work, in God's way, will never lack of God's support."

Please pray for the church in China.

16

SUFFERING BUT VICTORIOUS

SHANGHAI, CHINA, MARCH 2019

It was a cold morning when my Dragon Air flight from Hong Kong landed at Shanghai Pudong Airport in China. As is standard procedure now, I walked up to the automatically controlled immigration gate and slid my China Home Return Permit into the digital scanner. Usually, the door opens right up and lets me through. But this time, it did not. Instead, a red light came on and an immigration officer walked up. He looked at some information on his tablet for several minutes. Then he said:

"Sir, please give me your permit. You need to come with me, and another officer will need to talk to you."

"Hi sir," I asked, *"What is the problem?"*

"I do not know," was his only answer.

He led me to a small interview room, where he told me to wait for the other officer. I sat there by myself, wondering what the issue could be. I began to pray, "Lord, please help me! I know this is not good. I have experienced short detentions and questionings many times, and every time You get me out of trouble. Please help me again! Lord, I do not want to spend my time in prison in China, but Your will be done. If I have to, please give me the courage to tell the truth. If I have to suffer, please give me the physical, mental, and spiritual strength to endure all the unexpected difficulties. Let me continue to bring glory to You!"

I knew it was usual for the officers to keep me waiting for at least half an hour. It was a difficult time as my mind thought about all the different possibilities, the worst of which was imprisonment with no release date and separation from my family and friends.

I had my phone and my backpack, but I didn't send out any messages while sitting there because the officers could force me to hand over my phone and examine all my messages. In fact, I had three phones in China so that I could use one for sensitive information, and hand officers another phone with no information on it (the third phone was a spare, in case of emergencies). But here, they could search my belongings and find all the phones.

After twenty-five long minutes, two young immigration officers entered the room. When I looked closer at the patches on their uniforms, I realized they were not immigration officers, but National Security Police officers. One of them asked:

"Well, Mr. Young, you are from Hong Kong, right?"

"Yes," I replied.

"Please come with me," he said, as he motioned for me to follow him out of the room.

They led me to a slightly bigger room with a table and computer monitor. They sat on one side of the table, while I sat on the other side. The older of the two officers asked:

"Mr. Young, you come to China quite often, almost every month, sometimes twice every month. What are you doing here?"

I prepare myself for this question every time I travel into China. I prepare myself to tell the truth and refuse to lie to them. I will tell them I am a Christian and a pastor. I travel into China to do some teaching and meet with my pastor friends and church brothers and sisters. But I will never give names or locations to them.

I was about to answer, when the older officer suddenly leaned over to the younger officer, whispering quietly that he needed to use the restroom. Although he whispered, I heard him because the room was so small and quiet. He left, leaving me alone with the younger officer.

The younger officer looked at me and said:

"Teacher An, I know who you are!"

I was shocked, but I knew instantly to keep my composure and hide my feelings. I didn't change expressions or say anything. I knew it could be a trick. He continued:

"My mother, relatives, and friends have attended your trainings! They all said you are a good teacher. I cannot talk much, but I have a higher authority than the other officer. I can let you go now. I will handle the situation."

Before I could reply, he handed me my permit.

"Go, leave quickly before he comes back. I know his stomach is not feeling well today."

I left the room full of joy, and made my way out of the airport, which is quite large, in less than five minutes. As I was walking out of the airport, and then riding in the taxi, I kept praising my Lord. How wonderful He is to save me one more time. I was very close to prison, but once again, and not knowing why, I am free! The wind and rain will not hinder my service to the house churches. Incredible adventures happen outside my comfort zone. I also know now how I shall pray the next time I am in a situation like that—I will pray that someone needs to go to the restroom because of stomach problems!

I met with Pastor H in a large city in central China, but we actually met twenty feet apart, and acted as though we didn't know each other. We had previously communicated through our phones with special codes. Now, Pastor H was going to guide me to Pastor Y, who had just been released from prison.

I had known Pastor Y for six years, since I began working full-time with the house churches in China. He had been in prison for the gospel five times, each time for two to five years. His wife said he was in prison more than he was at home. Amazingly, his house churches continued to grow. He had no growth or funding strategies for his churches. He didn't even know when he would be arrested next, but he was dedicated to the gospel. Because of Pastor Y's heart to serve, and willingness to suffer for the gospel, the Lord blessed his churches, and they continued to grow.

Sometimes, joking with myself, I realize many of my new friends in China are prisoners — prisoners for the gospel. I have been so busy with ministries in China over the last twenty-some years, that I have lost contact with many of my Hong Kong friends. So many of my new friends are in prison.

After Pastor H and I met, I followed him on foot, walking for more than an hour in the hot, May weather. We walked through the suburbs of the city and into the countryside, always staying apart and never talking. There were no houses, only wheat fields. No one was working because it was close to noon. It was the best time to come, because anyone watching Pastor Y would be away for lunch.

Pastor H left a piece of paper on the ground and quickly walked away. I picked it up and read:

> *"Walk straight ahead for another twenty minutes. You should be able to see Y sleeping in the field. Stay short. Go quickly. Do not contact me until you are in another city. Be careful. Y is still being watched."*

I tore the paper into small pieces and let the wind scatter them.

I wore a green jacket to match the color of the field. I also had a brown hat to cover up some of my face, because I didn't look like a farmer from these villages. I walked as quickly as I could for about fifteen minutes. Then I saw someone lying very still in a field near a small pond. I walked up and hardly recognized Pastor Y. He was very skinny after three years in prison. He was lying on the muddy ground, with only a few pieces of newspaper as his mattress, sheet, and blanket. (This was the first time I learned that the newspaper *China Daily* was so useful!).

Pastor Y looked at me with tears coming out from his eyes. I wanted to help him up and give him a hug. He said:

> *"Teacher An, I cannot believe you will come to see someone like me, who is unworthy in this world! You cannot stay long! I know I am being watched. Even my wife and family cannot visit me now because my wife serves at the church full time. If she comes to visit me here, then she will be arrested."*

> *"Pastor Y, you are my hero! You are a faithful servant of God. I wish I could have your resume when I get to heaven, willing to suffer for our Lord. You carry your cross to follow Christ every day. I respect you very much. Do remember me when we meet in heaven. May I sit for a while and give you a hug, my dear brother?"*

Pastor Y replied with a weak voice:

> *"Do not touch me. My left arm and leg are kind of broken. The police released me from prison and put me on this field, so that I will not die in prison!"*

I began to cry.

> *"Don't worry, Pastor An! Please keep praying for me. As soon as I recover, I will go and share the gospel again. I will plant more churches for our Lord's kingdom!"*

> *"Pastor Y, I am supposed to come here to bring comfort to you, but you are encouraging me by your zeal to trust our Lord Jesus Christ!"*

> *"Teach An, thank you so much for taking care of my family financially when I was in prison. What breaks my heart is*

that when I suffer, my whole family suffers. However, your prayers and support comfort me and help my whole family to know that Jesus never forgets us. Thank you!"

"I will do my best to support you, your family, and your ministry. Many Christians outside of China care for you and are praying for you."

We prayed together, and then I had to leave before we were spotted. Two months later, I met with Pastor Y in another city with his family. He was still recovering, but was on his feet again proclaiming the gospel.

Pastor Y is just one of the faithful servants of God in China. God has chosen and trained many of His faithful servants in China to proclaim the gospel. That is why the church in China is a suffering but also victorious church. In the midst of suffering, I can see a harvest happening in China that is miraculous, incredible, and astounding.

———————————

Another year, also in May, I visited another house church pastor in central China. He planted three to four churches every year, with at least fifty new believers in each church. He had just been released from prison after serving two years for illegal church gatherings.

When I entered his home, which also served as the very first house church he planted, I saw almost no furniture except a wooden podium, some wooden stools, a couple of cabinets, and a bookshelf for a few Bibles and hymnals. He said:

"Teacher An, thank you for coming to a poor town like this. I do not even have a comfortable chair for you to sit on. I am so sorry. This is my home, and it has been raided four times in the last eight years. All my furniture and cooking equipment have been taken away with nothing left behind! Thank you for supporting my family when I was in prison. My church continues to grow without me. It is amazing

and all by the grace of our Lord!"

"It is great to know that you are out of prison, and our Lord will bless you for your willingness to suffer for the gospel. He will provide for your ministry! I am so sorry that you lost all your possessions every time your home was raided!"

"It does not matter now! I am getting used to it. God has a plan for me. Every time my furniture was taken away, I had to learn how to make furniture for my home and the church. After the fourth time, God made me a good carpenter like Jesus!"

To experience such joy in suffering is difficult for someone like me, who has lived most of my life in a free world, to understand. But I am learning.

I thank God for granting me the opportunity to work closely with the House Church of China for more than twenty years. My spiritual eyes are open to see how God works. I know my opposition, but more importantly, I know whom I trust and I know from where my strength comes. Obedience means respecting the sovereignty of another person, and I keep learning to be obedient to my Lord Jesus Christ because He is the King of all Kings!

What do I offer my King? I offer myself! I will be obedient to my King and will do whatever He asks me to do. I will give myself, and leave nothing left!

I will gladly give all I have for your souls. 2 Corinthians 12:15 (BBE)

我也甘心樂意的. 為你們的靈魂. 費財費力. 林後 12:15

We are witnessing the greatest evangelistic movement in the history of Christianity in China.

EPILOGUE:
THE SOUND OF SILENCE

Silence refers to submission to other people and a tendency to follow others. It also refers to the inability of people to communicate with each other, which is a good description of me when I was young. Facing my adoptive mother was like facing the communists: I did not dare to say anything. I kept my mouth shut and kept silent. Not because I wanted to, but because I was trying to protect myself.

In 1967, I traveled to Kowloon by train every day, for one hour and fifteen minutes each way, because I was attending a middle school in the city. That year, the famous movie *The Graduate* was released in the U.S. It was released in Hong Kong in 1969, and the song "The Sound of Silence" became very popular. During those days, almost every home had a radio. I was able to listen to radio programs when my adoptive mother was not home, and I can still remember a few of the lyrics:

And in the naked light I saw
Ten thousand people, maybe more
People talking without speaking
People hearing without listening
People writing songs that voices never share
And no one dared
Disturb the sound of silence[ix]

My last year in middle school was in 1969. Most students in Hong Kong knew some English, because Hong Kong was a British colony until 1997. My whole class would sing "The Sound of Silence" during recess, and we all knew it was written and performed by Simon and Garfunkel.

We did not understand the meaning of the song at all. We sang it because it was stylish to sing English songs. It was not until I was in college in 1995, when the internet became popular, that I was able to search for this song on the internet, and learned that it was written by Paul Simon in the aftermath of John F. Kennedy's assassination in 1963.

I like this song because when I was young, I was not talkative, and only said a few sentences per week, until I began working full-time at the age of fifteen. Even today, I still like to be alone, and I like silence. *People hearing without listening* is real, and this song lyric has always helped me to listen instead of just hearing the "noise."

I never went to any movies when I was growing up, but I walked past a cinema every day on my way home from school. I still remember the big poster for *The Graduate*, both in Chinese and English. There was a sentence on the poster that I wrote down and kept until now:

This is Benjamin—He's a little worried about his future.

When I graduated from high school in the summer of 1972 (before I became a Christian at the summer camp), I had big worries about my future. I did not know what to do. I wanted to continue my education, but my adoptive mother asked me to work to make more money for her. But I did not know what kind of job I could do. I was very depressed.

However, I only worried for two weeks, because that's when I became a Christian. From that point on, I knew who held my future. My worry was gone, and I started to learn how to trust my Lord. Even to this day, I do not make plans for myself. I do not need lots of money to retire, because I want to give it all to my Lord. He will take care of me.

When I was a little boy, I was afraid of darkness. I liked silence, but not silence in the dark. As I am an older man now, I know most people do not want to admit when they are old. Sometimes being old means we are stubborn, slow moving, and our engine need to be fixed. It is hard to come out of this darkness when we know death comes very near to us. If you are a little worried about your future, Jesus is the answer.

Jesus said, "I am the light of the world" (John 9:5). Only God can proclaim that in Himself there is no darkness. With light, I can clearly see the road in front of me. When I know where I am going, with the Light of the World leading me, I am certain of my future. It makes me more emotionally stable because I feel secure. Jesus has taught me to use my heart more than my brain. I have learned how to let others see and feel the love of Jesus through me. Sometimes I want to give up because I think I am hitting a dead end, but God always shows me

His way. The Holy Spirit also encourages me not to give up. More importantly, I know Jesus never gives up on me.

I wish I had become a Christian when I was five years old. I lost ten years of love and blessings from my Lord! When you love people, you want their heart, and I know Jesus wants my heart because He loves me.

I know in my life, many times, I probably did not do anything wrong, but I know I did not do the right thing. I know that even when I am wrong and sinful, like the prodigal son, Father God will hug me anytime I go home.

Life is a living sermon. This book is not a novel. It is not a sermon. It is a book of true stories, which have taught me to be a living sermon. I pray that my Lord will continue to help me live a life bigger than just my words.

Jesus can help us when we come to Him. If you are not a Christian and you have read this book, I pray that you will know how wonderful Jesus is. I pray that you will be completely at peace with God. Jesus loves you. His love has no bottom line.

Be blessed!

MY FAVORITE HYMN FROM THE HOUSE CHURCH OF CHINA

God's Presence is Here!
這裡有神的同在
(With Pinyin & Translation)

这 里 有 神 的 同 在，这 里 有 神 的 言 语，
zhe li you shen de tong zai, zhe li you shen de yan yu
God's presence is here, God's Word is here

这 里 有 圣 灵 的 恩 膏，这 里 是 另 一 个 天 地，
zhe li you sheng ling de en gao, zhe li shi ling yi ge tian di
The Spirit's blessing is here, this is a different world

看 哪 弟 兄 和 陆 同 居， 何 等 的 善 何 等 的 美
kan na di xiong he lu tong ju, he deng de shan he deng de mei
Look, how the brothers dwell among each other, how virtuous and beautiful

如 同 那 黑 门 的 甘 露， 降 在 锡 安 山 地，
ru tong na hei men de gan lu, jiang zai xi an shan di
As if the dew of Hermon were falling on Mount Zion

爱 在 这 里, 和 平 在 这 里,
ai zai zhe li,   he ping zai zhe li
Love is here, peace is here

光   明   在 这 里, 生 命 在 这 里,
guang ming zai zhe li, sheng ming zai zhe li
The light is here, life is here

耶 和 华 所 命 定 的 福 都 在 这 里,
ye he hua suo ming ding de fu dou zai zhe li
The blessing that the Lord designates is here

你 若 想 要 得 到 他, 在 耶 稣 基 督 里。
ni ruo xiang yao de dao ta, zai ye su ji du li
Should you want to receive Him, you must do so through Christ

A PHOTOGRAPHIC PORTRAIT OF THE AUTHOR THROUGH ZEISS LENSES

Endorsements from Friends, Chinese Pastors and Staff Members.
Endorsements are listed in no particular order.

These are my witnesses, and I am circled by so great a cloud of witnesses (Heb. 12). They are part of my life, and have accompanied me through different seasons. Many thanks to them.

(The Zeiss Lens, which is made in Germany, is one of the best professional camera lenses in the world. When I was a young photographer, I loved Zeiss lenses, although I never owned one since they were so expensive.)

HONG KONG FRIENDS

I am privileged to be invited to write an endorsement for Barnabas' new book, a book that shares his work and ministry in China for the sake of Jesus Christ. It is indeed an exceptional honor for me.

My wife Grace and I have known Barnabas and Margaret for almost half a century. We grew up together in the same youth group at church, and got to know one another very well.

Barnabas is a very special person. He is quiet and works very seriously. He is unafraid of difficulties, and had the foresight to envision great things since the beginning. Perhaps that had to do with his upbringing and experiences.

We all held different hopes and dreams toward our futures when we were young, hoping that we could contribute positively toward our society, country, people group, and Christ's heavenly kingdom. I remember at the time, when we were sharing about our goals in life, Barnabas assuredly and boldly said, "I must work toward opening the door for the gospel in China for Christ." To be perfectly honest, it was the mid-1970s at the time, during the height of the Cultural Revolution. The Open Door Policy and the reforms it brought had yet to be enacted, and there were many young people who shared the same zeal to save our country and our people. However, rare was the man who actually followed through and devoted his life toward that goal.

During the 1980s, we were all busy with work and taking care of our young children. Although that left less time for us to socialize at church, Barnabas and I maintained a profound and brotherly relationship. Our children also grew up together and remain close friends to this day.

The events of June 4 in 1989 brought our lives even closer, as we went on the streets together protesting for the democracy and freedom of China, accusing those in the Beijing government of massacring the students at Tiananmen, then migrating abroad . . . these events have forever changed the lives of our generation.

In the mid-90s, when we all reached middle age and sought more stability in our lives, Barnabas brought his entire family to the United States to fulfill his dream of obtaining a higher education. Through time and effort devoted toward his studies, he was equipped and prepared by the Lord to fulfill His calling in China. While others looked at Barnabas with skepticism, I deeply believed and supported his decision. This is indeed the Barnabas that I knew for years.

After ten years or so, Barnabas came back to Asia and shared with us his new calling (old goal): to serve Christians in China. We were greatly touched by his utter devotion toward Jesus.

We also became prayer partners and brought our needs before the Lord. Barnabas would share details of his ministry in China on occasion, and we were greatly encouraged by the testimony of those who serve Him in China.

Today, Barnabas has taken time to organize his experiences and encounters in ministry as well as his thoughts into a book. He serves as a fine example for those of us who don't work in ministry full-time.

> *"For it is God who works in you to will and to act in order to fulfill his good purpose." "Then you will shine among them like stars in the sky as you hold firmly to the Word of Life. And then I will be able to boast on the day of Christ that I did not run or labor in vain." (Phil. 2:13, 16)*

May the Lord richly bless and accept the ministry of Brother Barnabas. Amen!

—RANDY NG
Businessman

———————

Barnabas' autobiography depicts his story of following the teachings of Jesus, and is a testament to a faithful Christian serving God throughout his life. It portrays Barnabas' journey in consecrating his life to Christ and fulfilling the Great Commission, his dedication to cultivating gospel followers, and his perseverance in caring for the lost.

There is an ancient Chinese proverb that illustrates the countless hardships Barnabas endured throughout his childhood—"Honing gives a sharp edge to a sword, and bitter cold adds keen fragrance to a plum blossom." Today, his work is dedicated to serving God persistently, in any workplace and any country.

> *"Give thanks in all circumstances; for this is God's will for you in Christ Jesus." (1 Thess. 5:18)*

—TIMON WONG
Over forty years of brotherhood with Barnabas and his family
Residing in Toronto, Canada since 1997
Hong Kong family friend

The Torchbearer.

"How beautiful are the feet of those who bring good news!"
(Romans 10:15)

Barnabas and I first met each other at church youth fellowship back in Hong Kong around 1978, a good forty-two years ago! We grew up and served not only in the same fellowship, but belonged to the same cell group.

During those much younger years, together with a number of others, we shared many happy and memorable moments, such as jogging, barbecue, stargazing, camping, and enjoying late supper after Saturday evening fellowship gatherings. The sharing of aspirations on life and the mutual encouragement in Christ during those early years of my Christian life had a lasting impact on me!

As of Barnabas, I always hold him dearly, not only as one of my few lifelong buddies, but also as one of my few elder brothers-in-Christ. Though he is not someone of many words, he is caring and trustworthy, but most admirably, remains steadfastly faithful to his calling in serving Him!

Barnabas and I have been living worlds apart since my move to Sydney, Australia more than twenty-six years ago. Over these years, he has been tirelessly bringing the gospel to His people and equipping the Lord's faithful workers through his ministries.

Thankfully, over the years, we and the other few lifelong buddies have been able to catch up regularly! Whenever we do so, we are all amazed and inspired by how the Lord works through him and protects him!

Thanks to Barnabas for so generously sharing his life stories with us. Journey with him and you will find that he has certainly committed his life to the Lord to build up His people and church, despite everything that came his way.

Pray that our Almighty God keep and bless Barnabas and his fellow coworkers, that they continue to bring light and His Hope to all those they serve, despite all the dangers that have been so often looming over them!

—ANGUS TSE

An amazing life journey full of God's blessings, grace, mercy, miracles, and companionship, when Barnabas follows the Lord humbly to fulfill God's perfect will in his life. Barnabas is a godly man who walks in faith and trusts the Lord for guidance in bringing the lost souls in China to Christ. Barnabas' writing style is warm and engaging. Thank you, Barnabas, for inspiring me to seek God more fully and sharing your book with us.

—VIVIAN HON

If you consider yourself a common person but don't want to live commonly like many others, then I would strongly recommend you to read this autobiography of Barnabas. This is a good read and you can get some light and encouragement from it.

—STEPHEN WU
48-year-old friend to author
Senior Management
Maersk Shipping Industry

This book records a pastor's life of ministry. He revisits his life's journey with his readers, as one of those "*who have been called according to his purpose*" (Romans 8:28) and the actualization of "*God's handiwork*" (Ephesians 2:10). Through Barnabas' obedience to God and constant readiness in responding to

God's call, he shares God's grace with those around him through his life and work. He ceaselessly lives out the gospel so that we may better understand God's love, bravery, humility, nobility, and loyalty.

Barnabas has utterly devoted his life to serving the body of Christ in China without reservation, and has worked tirelessly for decades. For that, he has earned my profound respect. I most admire Barnabas' work in encouraging those who are struggling or weak in Christ, and leading them out of their difficulties and despair. He doesn't care about the (often negative) association, and leads them fully before the Lord. He does not boast and serves quietly and humbly. However, when he does speak on the pulpit, he speaks with God's righteousness and truth, not attracting the congregation to him through his charisma, but rather bringing everyone to submit before the power and might of God's Word.

I have known Barnabas for over thirty years, and the one thing I'm most touched by is his fatherly and accommodating heart. There is a Chinese saying that states, "*Hundreds of rivers flow into the ocean, for the ocean is big enough to accept them,*" which means to encounter the world with a broad and accommodating attitude. It is easy to say but difficult to do. Barnabas lives this daily, and he leads and pastors his flock with love. In his book, Barnabas has mentioned his ordinary nature numerous times, as God was the one who has selected, molded, equipped, and sent him out to be a shepherd of God's pleasing. This book chronicles a humble and steadfast life. To God be the glory!

—JUMBO YU

———————

It is very difficult to find simple and apt words to describe Barnabas.

He is my spiritual teacher. Like the countless house churches that he works with, I only get to see him once or twice a year, as he is indeed a very busy man. I consider any time that I get to spend with Barnabas a blessing and privilege. For me, it is the quality, rather than the quantity of time that we spend together that is most precious. He listens to me patiently, makes a few important points, and kindly reminds me to lift my prayers first and foremost to Christ, He who is most important in my life!

"For it is by grace you have been saved, through faith – and this is not from yourselves, it is the gift of God – not by works, so that no one can boast." (Ephesians 2:8-9)

Words alone cannot fully convey the adventurous life that Barnabas has led. However, if you simply employ a bit of imagination and empathy, you can begin to comprehend the loneliness of his youth, the impact of the gospel upon his life, his steadfast loyalty towards God, as well as the love he has for his wife.

Through the life of Barnabas, we learn that our God is not silent, but actively engages with our lives. However, we must learn to quiet our restless hearts and wait upon the Lord to hear His voice:

"Yes, my soul, find rest in God; my hope comes from Him." (Psalms 62:5)

—Pele Wong

———————

I have known Barnabas for more than fourteen years. God has blessed me with a period of time when I partnered with him in a training ministry. I have also had the privilege of serving Margaret's handicraft ministry in China, Hong Kong, and England. That provided me with a chance to learn from him to be a dedicated follower of Christ and to serve God humbly.

Many Christians do well in talking about their faith, but Barnabas also does well in living out his faith. His faith shines through his life and ministry, which has touched my heart profoundly.

His life stories in this book are snapshots of him and his ministry. They only show a small portion of his godly character and a glimpse of God's glory in his ministry. Even though he was deprived of love when he was young, he has given out a lot of love to many people whom he has met in his ministry for God. I think it is not difficult for you to learn from this book that Barnabas is a gracious person of humility, generosity, bravery, sincerity, and honesty. He has never failed to show his godly wisdom too.

This book is genuine, as is Barnabas, a faithful servant of God and a saint for our age.

—**SCARLET CHAN**
Chairwoman,
Walking With You Ministry

MAINLAND CHINESE PASTORS

This book recounts the birth and upbringing of Barnabas, along with the blessings he has received through his spiritual journey. He offered up his own life and his family to serve our country with over a billion souls, and the Lord has affirmed the fruits of his spirit. God has used Barnabas to bless tens of thousands of people, and I have been greatly blessed and encouraged by Barnabas as well. I pray and wish the same for you.

—**SNOWMAN**

This book records the life of a man who devoted his life toward faithful servanthood. Barnabas respects everyone he meets, and he holds God's truth in the highest regard. He constantly takes on risks to unfailingly serve the church in China. He is humble like Christ, and willing to move boldly into any situation and environment. He has traversed all across China, always giving love and blessings to others, while taking away their pain and difficulties. He is the mentor to countless pastors, and navigator to countless churches throughout China. Barnabas and his family are themselves a movement and exceptional unit, fully committed to serving the church in China. It has been my privilege to know Barnabas over the years. His words and deeds have spurred me on. His life and testimony are presented in this book, and I highly recommend giving it a read.

—震 ZHOU

———————

Barnabas is my spiritual father, as well as my example for how to serve. Although he and I don't actually exchange too many words when we meet in person, our hearts shall forever be aligned in Christ. Since 2009, I have learned many things from Barnabas every time we meet: humility, love, and steadfast servanthood. Everybody bears witness to his love and offering for the church in China, and it greatly encourages us. The church of China will continue to pray for Barnabas, and the Lord shall know and account for his sacrifice for China. May the Lord bless him and his family.

The first time I met Barnabas was in 2009, when he shared his burden for the countless souls of China. We have since met up many times, and his words, deeds, character, and integrity have greatly impacted me. His burden for the souls of China remains true and has never changed. If you read this book, you will surely learn of complete offering, responsibility, steadfast service, and never giving up regardless of difficulties encountered. May the Lord richly bless you through the life and testimony of Barnabas.

—南昌 ZHAO

Thank You Lord for introducing me to Barnabas, and that I can be a witness to his calling by God to fulfill His will—to serve and be a blessing to others. Barnabas has served the church in China for more than thirty years. He has remained consistent and unchanging in regards to his calling, and has steadfastly supported tens of thousands of God's faithful servants in China. Barnabas is a messenger of love, and he pays special attention to all those involved with the theological training and equipping of young people. His life and love have inspired and ignited many, many young people.

May the Lord bless this book, may every reader of this book also be inspired and ignited by Barnabas' life and testimony to love life, to save souls, to develop churches, and to fulfill the Great Commission of Christ.

—美 FENG

I have known this faithful servant of God for ten years. For years I have heard from many others of Barnabas' humility, his refinement through trials, and how he never gives up. I now see how he glorifies the Lord through his life and testimony, as illustrated in this book. This book recounts his difficult childhood and the story of his salvation, as "*we know that in all things God works for the good of those who love him, who have been called according to his purpose*" (Romans 8:28). Barnabas has worked tirelessly toward the cultivation of new churches and future church leaders in China. He is one who pleases the Lord, a learned and experienced steward for the church of China. May this book encourage and affirm all who read it.

—淑雲ZHAO

"Now Moses was a very humble man, more humble than anyone else on the face of the earth." (Numbers 12:3)

This verse of Scripture may be applied to Barnabas as well. He has truly achieved that through his work with the Chinese House Church, and his sense of duty and burden toward the House Church is indeed extraordinary and not easily replicated by others. He knows and understands us intricately, and he relinquishes his safety and worries in order to come to be among us and fellowship with us much like Jesus did. He has trained and mentored countless pastors, and has worked hard to resolve problems that pastors and church planters often face in China, encouraging us to continue God's work through us. He does not at all look down on those who are impoverished and uneducated, but instead gives even more patience and help to those, like me, who need it. As pastors and church planters from the Chinese House Church, we feel the love of Barnabas, his family, and his staff every time we attend one of his theological training seminars. Barnabas is truly a fine example for us. His contribution toward serving the Chinese House Church has been great over the years, and we trust that his rewards are indeed in heaven.

—菊 Hu

———————

Barnabas is a faithful servant employed by God. His life is rather extraordinary. From being an orphan, to becoming a great minister and missionary, every story he tells is a classic. I have been deeply touched by these stories countless times, and I trust that God will use these stories to reach you and impact your ministry. Barnabas has served the Chinese church faithfully over the years, and his heart is filled with love and burden for the Chinese church. He has had many encounters and stories throughout China over the years, all of them testifying to the power and grace of our God. I pray that you will reap the benefits and blessings from this book as I have.

—坤 Li

Barnabas has traversed through many cities and towns throughout China seeking God's truth. He cultivates genuine relationships with everyone he meets, and ensures the gospel and the living waters of Christ flow throughout China, nourishing the lands and His people. Barnabas is humble, wholly loyal and devoted. He has obeyed God's will for him all his life. He is a strong and living rock, serving as a foundation of the church in China. He offered his life as a living sacrifice for the Lord to serve the church in China for the rest of his days. He is a living encyclopedia volume, full of knowledge and wisdom for the benefit of others. Although he is past sixty years old, he continues to fight the beautiful fight without any indication or desire to retire from battle. He continues to walk the narrow road, and holds fast to his faith and the righteous crown of God. How can we remain idle after reading his testimony? This book is a precious gift from the Lord to you. May we benefit from its wisdom, apply it to our lives, and commit ourselves fully to the Lord. Amen.

—鵬 LIU

HC MINISTRY PASTORS & STAFF

I first met Barnabas in an orphanage in central China. He was invited by a mutual friend to lead his team and conduct a summer camp for the orphans at the orphanage. I was there as a volunteer, and I was greatly impacted by Barnabas and his team. He always worked and labored alongside his team. He did not at all flaunt his authority as leader, was approachable and warm, and paid great attention to details. At the time, I prayed for the opportunity to one day learn from such a leader. Praise God, He answered my prayer, and I indeed received the opportunity to join his organization and ministry. In these past ten years, I witnessed his love for his coworkers with my own eyes. In all that we do, whether running theological seminars, visiting partners, or other ministerial endeavors, he personifies joy and laughs often with us. Rarer still is his empathy and compassion for those who have endured hardships, mourning with them while offering care, encouragement, and tangible help. He develops and builds up those around him unreservedly. He often says his life is a life of receiving and experiencing God's grace, so he shares God's grace with others as well. He talks the talk, and then walks the walk. As Paul says in 1 Corinthians 4:15, "*Even if you had ten thousand guardians in Christ, you do not have many fathers.*" Barnabas is a rare man who possesses a fatherly heart and serves the church in China as a servant leader. I trust that like me, you too are greatly encouraged by God's mighty works detailed in Barnabas' book, and to learn from him, just as he learned from Jesus.

—JASMINE

If you must make an endorsement of someone, you must know this person very well. Although in order to know this person, you need to serve and work alongside him. We can observe someone's character through his daily ministry, through the extraordinary as well as the mundane.

I am very thankful that I've been able to serve alongside Barnabas throughout these years. Although there is a large age gap between us, he understands young people very well and the way we think. I'm also very grateful for Barnabas' help and encouragement in my personal life, as well as my ministerial life. He is my teacher and advisor, and he provides spiritual guidance as well as practical help when I encounter difficulties. When Barnabas gives you help, he does not limit your potential, but rather unleashes it by pushing you forward.

It is not easy to serve in ministry. You will meet many different sorts of people and not all of them are nice and good. It is a daily endeavor to learn to love our brothers and sisters and to serve them with the love of Christ. Barnabas serves as an example for us all, always reminding us to love those whom we serve, to love through deliberate and practical actions, particularly for those who are already serving tirelessly themselves. It is easy to seemingly convey love through simple words, but it is much more difficult to love through tangible action. I know Barnabas offers frequent support for the house church pastors and church planters throughout China in all sorts of ways, especially those who are under persecution and enduring financial difficulties. In decades past, he often forewent taking his salary and instead redirected that money to ministries throughout China. He would then take money from his personal savings and privately give to individual pastors and church planters who truly needed help. He has visited China often throughout the years, particularly to rural and remote villages that few outsiders visit, to care for these often forgotten pastors and congregations. He preaches and shares Scripture everywhere he goes in order to encourage and ignite the spirit of Chinese believers everywhere. There are great challenges serving the Chinese House Church. The environment in-country is highly against Christianity. Going into China as a Hong Konger serving the Chinese House Church guarantees political pressure and harassment. Only the love of Jesus can cover and relieve these pressures. He loves others through action. He is a respectable shepherd and a wonderful spiritual advisor. I know and understand Barnabas for I have worked alongside him for many years. I am most grateful for being able to serve God and his people alongside him on our journey of ministry. May the Lord bless him and his work, empowering him to better serve the church in China.

—Enoch

I am very blessed to be a part of the HC Ministry and to be actively involved with its ministries. Be it my spiritual walk or ministerial life, I have been greatly impacted by Barnabas and his ministry in ways that has transformed my life forever. In my encounters with Barnabas, he much prefers to serve God through concrete action rather than empty words. As I observe Barnabas' interactions with the Chinese pastors, he is always humble, sincere, and approachable with everyone regardless of their background. He is always patient with every pastor, listens intently to understand their circumstances, and does his best to help. Through observing Barnabas, I have learned of his active pursuit of God's calling for him, and his devotion to that calling. The Lord has brought forth tremendous blessings through the heart and work of Barnabas. Like Paul, Barnabas has taken time to record his calling, leading, and insights from the Lord through the written word. I am certain that you will be blessed by the Lord through Barnabas' words as well.

—KONG

I am very thankful that Barnabas' book will be published soon. This is a must-read for every person interested in the Chinese House Church. It is a precious resource of the historical development of the Chinese church, from the end of the twentieth century until now. Barnabas is not only a wise scholar, he is also a pastor who has walked alongside us through thick and thin throughout his tenure. He does not indulge in highbrow theories, and he does not engage in empty and impractical speech; he lives and serves humbly, as Christ has demonstrated before us. He has never disobeyed the vision that the Lord presented him. Rather, he responded to God's calling through fruitful actions in ministry.

I remember meeting Barnabas for the first time in the winter of 2000. It was in a small house in the outskirts of Beijing, and I had just dedicated my life to full-time ministry. Over the years, I have received tremendous blessing from God through Barnabas in both theological study as well as in active ministry. His personal testimony gave me great conviction and encouragement to faithfully follow the Lord's path for me.

Twenty years later, Barnabas no longer requires translation from Cantonese to Mandarin from his wife Margaret, and both of his sons assist him in his work. Over the years, Barnabas has truly lived out the verse, "*As for me and my household, we will serve the Lord*" (Joshua 24:15). His willingness to work alongside the Chinese House Church and openly chronicle its history is bold and humbling. Most people in his position would downplay the association. Barnabas is someone who could have relied on his own talent, work ethic, and resources to build a bigger organization, to bask in the praise and admiration of many, or to avoid taking on political and personal risks. Instead, he has steadfastly and humbly served the Chinese House Church without fanfare, cultivating relationships and trust with many house church movements and leaders, aiding the movements' development, and counseling the leaders. He has earned the love and respect of all those he serves. It is God's blessing for Barnabas to have this opportunity to compile his precious encounters throughout China over the years into a book, so that we can witness God's unceasing work in China. This book is not written for profit or fame, but as a testament of God's love toward His people and the love of His people for one another. It encourages us to stand firm in the salvation of Christ in spite of danger, outright ridicule, and persecution, without complaint or regret.

May Barnabas' searing heart continue to burn for the sake of the gospel, to be used by God to warm the souls of many, and to impact them to faithfully serve our Lord. May more people walk this glorious path of salvation through faith.

—TEACHER GUO

———————————

Barnabas is a well-known and well-regarded servant amongst brothers and sisters in the Chinese House Church. I myself have known Barnabas for many years as well. His unadorned and humble character, deep love of the Lord, and industriousness in ministry have all left an indelible impression on me. His testimony has greatly impacted my life and ministry.

It is a great honor for me to write this endorsement for his new book.

If you would like to know what God has done through the church in China over the past few decades, please read this book because the author of this book has witnessed and partaken in His work.

If you want to be a true believer and follower of Christ, please read this book because the author uses his own life to illustrate the contribution and sacrifice necessary in order to follow Christ.

If you would like to be successful in the eyes of God, please read this book for you will be inspired as to how God defines success:

> Barnabas is a successful husband. He and Margaret have spent decades together through thick and thin, remaining faithful to God and to one another. It is a marriage founded in the love and example of Christ;

> Barnabas is a successful father. To have your own sons serving alongside you in ministry is the most successful ministry;

> Barnabas is a successful leader. He is always praying, supporting, and encouraging everyone to tread forward in our heavenly pursuits.

I wish you the best as you embark on this journey with Barnabas. May you be greatly blessed.

—TEACHER MARK

I was first introduced to Barnabas by my pastor on August 16, 2012. I soon joined his ministry and eight years have since passed. He is my spiritual leader, but he's more like my father that possesses the great love of Christ. Through the life of Barnabas, I am able to witness the life that God wants us to lead. When I was weak and lacking in faith, he was the one who comforted me and encouraged me. He loves others through action and has made a profound impact not only on me but also my family. Everything he does exudes God's love, glorifying His name through his daily work. Through his life and testimony, my entire family was brought before the Lord. I am most thankful for meeting Barnabas and getting to know him — truly my good spiritual father. Words alone cannot fully convey my gratefulness for him. Thank you!

—LEANNE

———————

As his spiritual junior, I am grateful to get to know Barnabas and his life story. I am also thankful to be able to work alongside him in ministry, serving the Chinese House Church. He has brought great encouragement and conviction to me and my colleagues, who are of a younger generation, and has become our example.

In my years working alongside Barnabas, I have witnessed his hands-on work ethic and the humble attitude in which he serves. He is a living example for us to learn from. If you are a young person in ministry such as me, you will most likely feel the same as me as I read through this book. The road of servanthood is filled with weeds and thorns, but when we observe that our spiritual elder submits himself fully for Christ and the gospel without hesitation and doubt, we strive to emulate the way he lives his life, and the Lord has blessed us through Barnabas.

—JONATHAN

———————

Barnabas is a faithful servant whose life is pleasing to the Lord. He has led his whole family to serve the Chinese House

Church, and they have all made sacrifices in their ministry. Barnabas has helped countless house churches, as well as the brothers and sisters in them. That includes me: I have worked alongside Barnabas and Margaret for seventeen years, and they have helped me tremendously in these past seventeen years. Like my colleagues, I am most thankful for a leader like Barnabas, who possesses a kind father's heart. He has earned the respect of brothers and sisters throughout China. He commits everything to the Lord and faithfully serves Him daily. Thank You Lord for letting me know Barnabas, who is both fatherly and brotherly at once. He has followed God's calling and served the Chinese House Church faithfully for decades. Not everyone is capable and willing to do this. His love comes from the Lord, a love that transcends circumstances, that confirms and convicts the sons and daughters who serve Him. It is this love that encourages me daily to pursue God's calling for me.

—TIN

———————

Different people have different pursuits: there are those who spend their whole lives seeking after fame and success. There are those who seek peace and quiet. Then there are those who seek after God's will and act upon it.

I have known Barnabas for almost thirty years. He was the executive director of a Christian camp and had already begun planting churches in the mainland. He later went to study in the United States while maintaining his ministerial efforts in China, eventually obtaining an MBA degree. However, rather than joining the world of business, he returned here and continued to serve the Chinese House Church. He spent years traveling to small villages and towns throughout China to care for and minister to countless brothers and sisters, and willingly took on the risks of potentially being arrested, questioned, and imprisoned.

Barnabas was an orphan born into difficult circumstances. The

Lord trained and refined him to draw strength from Him and remain faithful in his words and deeds. This is all part of God's beautiful will, as the Potter shapes His clay into instruments that suit His purpose. Barnabas also leads his whole family and staff to serve China together.

Barnabas has recorded his life story and has now written a book. I pray that readers of this book may learn of God's amazing will and power through this faithful servant of God. Through the testimony and ministry of Barnabas, we are indeed witnesses to God's mighty work in China.

Countless lives which have been transformed by Christ's sacrifice upon the cross, now actively take up their crosses and follow Christ, enduring tribulation and trials while bringing forth a fierce wind of revival throughout China and other parts of the world.

—Phoebe

If you ask me what a "servant leader" is, I will introduce you to Barnabas. As both a leader and elder, he not only teaches with words but also with action, being hands-on with his ministry and leading by example. He is indeed our example and benchmark.

If you ask me what "gentle humility" is, I will also introduce you to Barnabas, for he finds stillness in God's presence, listens to His voice, and seeks after His will. He follows the example of Christ, to humbly serve those around him with action.

If you ask me what "passionate servanthood" is, I will again introduce you to Barnabas, for he serves others with all the time and energy he has.

You will be able to find truthful evidence to all of Barnabas' qualities that I have listed in his book.

—Grace

I was blessed to have the opportunity to study and be trained at one of the HC Ministry's seminaries, and I've been working and serving with this ministry ever since I graduated. I am most grateful to have heard Barnabas' testimony and observe the mighty work that God has done in his life. The Lord does not call those who are capable, wealthy, or knowledgeable, but rather those who are willing to be shaped and molded by Him to impact and change the world. As I reflect on why we serve the way we do, as well as the value, purpose, and meaning of it all, I'm privileged to witness the pastors that attend our training seminars and how they're touched and transformed by the Lord. That's when I know that God uses Barnabas to be a blessing to China. As I serve alongside Barnabas, I am encouraged by his selfless love for the churches in China. He teaches us to care about people, to meet their needs, and to serve with love, as Christ has done for us.

—CHRISTY

Barnabas is always hands-on with his work, can see through all matters big and small, and gives his all.

From his beginnings at his home church by the seaside, to his travels visiting churches across China, he shows that God's love is boundless.

From working at numerous ministries, to founding his own to serve those he is called to serve, he shows his humble obedience.

From upper-class urban areas to rural, impoverished villages, he serves everyone equally, and he shows that God's Word is in his heart.

We can witness God working through Barnabas in everything he does. We can see God's love emanating from Barnabas through his commitment to serve God's people.

I sincerely recommend this book to everyone, to get to know this pastor who has offered his entire life for Christ. May this book be an encouragement to you, to rely on God more and to be ever more faithful to Him.

—JEREMIAH

———————

Barnabas is a pastor and servant who emulates the life of Christ. He started his ministry from his fishing village church, then served at a youth camp for over two decades, and started his ministry in China full-time after that. He closely follows Christ with his every step, and does not do things for himself but rather for the glory of God and to build up others.

Through this book, Barnabas details the history of God's work on his life. He also reveals God's plan for His church in China. Although Barnabas has encountered many difficulties and trials, he serves and relies upon a victorious God, who guides him through these trials. I believe through Barnabas' personal testimony and what the Lord has done in his life, we may receive comfort, strength, and encouragement.

—KRIS

———————

When you read an autobiography such as this, you may have the following question: just who, indeed, is Barnabas?

You may know him, or you may not. But that is not the most important thing. For after you finish reading this book, you can see how God shapes and molds his faithful servants into His capable vessels in order to receive His divine calling and accomplish His Word. I believe this is what is meant by Ephesians 2:10:

> "For we are God's handiwork, created in Christ Jesus to do good works, which God prepared in advance for us to do."

If you carry the burden for the Great Commission, this book

records how the Lord has led Barnabas to serve the church of China. He will share with you many stories and thoughts in regards to his ministry in China, the testimonies of many faithful servants of the Chinese House Church, and the many miracles that God has performed not only in his life but also throughout China. It is my wish that through this book, you will not only come to a deeper understanding of the realities that Chinese believers face on a daily basis, but also witness the qualities that the servants of God possess. May you be convicted and encouraged as we continue to carry out the Great Commission together.

—KELVIN

———————

We often say that one life impacts another; I think this applies perfectly to Pastor Barnabas, who is my boss at work as well as my father figure.

I know that the Lord called him to do one thing ever since he was young: "Serve the Chinese House Church." He was committed to that calling then, and he continues to labor vigorously toward this calling until this very day. His understanding of the Chinese House Church is greater than many brothers and sisters who *grew up* in the Chinese House Church, for he is no mere spectator from afar, but rather someone who leads us from amongst our ranks and serves alongside us. He often sits in a car for many hours, traveling deep into the mountains and rural areas to meet and encourage believers there. Although the current political situation in China is tenuous at best, Barnabas has never ceased his work and support for the Chinese House Church.

As my superior at work, he holds himself as accountable as everyone else. He is approachable, and he works right alongside us. He allows us freedom to be creative and express ourselves in our work, as long as we adhere to the inherent core values and biblical principles as believers.

I have known many pastors in my life and work. There truly aren't many pastors who have sons and daughters working with them. Barnabas serves China with his wife and two sons. Knowing Barnabas and his sons, they all could have gotten much higher-paying jobs in other fields, but instead they all chose to commit their lives to serve the Chinese House Church. One life truly impacts another, as the sons follow the example of their father. Barnabas is also a spiritual father to all of the staff. While he doesn't talk much and prefers to lead by example, when he does speak, it is always to encourage us and build us up.

Thank You Lord, for blessing me with a pastor, boss, and spiritual father like Barnabas. May the Lord bless him and his family, and may his walk with Christ receive blessings upon blessings and strength upon strength!

—JOYCE

I was blessed to work on Barnabas' staff for four years, and saw firsthand how he lives according to God's Word and the specific calling he's been given. His love for Christ and the Chinese house churches really define who he is as a person, and his humility attests to the work of the Holy Spirit in his life. There's nobody I know who has had so many incredible mountaintop life experiences, yet speaks about them from such a selfless, "all the glory to God" type of perspective. My life was forever changed through the time I spent working alongside this man, and I believe those who read his testimony in these pages will be blessed in a similar way.

—KENDAL STOLTZFUS

Many years ago, I witnessed Barnabas' selfless love and endless work for the House Church on my first visit inside China. Afterwards, I had more opportunities to visit house churches and underground Bible schools with Barnabas. The experience was life changing. The fearless faith of Chinese Christians in the face of overwhelming opposition and oppression led me to join the HC Ministry and work full-time for several years. I have never known a Christian man or worked with a ministry so authentically Christian and tirelessly faithful to helping those in need. I know this book will encourage you as it has me. I also hope *Leave Nothing Left* will spiritually unite you in the struggles of our brothers and sisters in China.

—D, HC Ministry Worker

FAMILY

Shakespeare said, "*Love is not to see with eyes but to see with heart.*" Jesus Christ embraces everyone with love, but communism sees everyone as the enemy. Communism tries to create class struggles and stir up differences between classes. This is not what family is all about. Without love, it is not a family.

I did not have a family until 1981, when I married my wife Margaret. I had no family background. I started fresh when I got married. When I didn't know what to do with my marriage, I went to Jesus. He was my first audience. When I had my own son, I needed to learn how to hold a little baby in my arms. I had to learn much from scratch.

God gave me a very different career path. I became a freshman in college when I was thirty-nine years old. I brought my whole family with me to the United States, because I would not leave my family behind to pursue my own dream.

When my sons were teenagers, I was just like a fireman; when they needed me, I would show up in three minutes. Now that they have their own friends and families, my role is a cheerleader, and I disappear when they need their space. My wife and I will not ask them to meet with us every week or for a fixed period of time. We are all completely free. Love cannot be forced, but I know they love me.

Regarding my wife and my marriage, we are spending our life together until we go to heaven. But according to the Bible, sons and daughters will leave home and form their own families. I am not going to make a mistake by loving my sons, daughters-in-law, and grandchildren more than my wife. Many families have problems because they confuse themselves with whom they should love the most.

I have asked my family to share with you about our family and our ministry, and have not told them what to share. It is all from their hearts.

_____

Forty-five years ago, on a dark and windy evening, I spent my first night at the Christian camp in Hong Kong. Since I was a brand new member of staff, I was curious about everything.

By then, most of the lights were turned off and it was pitch black. However, that only spurred me on to explore the camp further. After walking in the dark for a while, I took a brief rest. Suddenly, I saw a light turn on and off again in one of the rooms. A light being turned on and off inside a room is not fascinating in itself, but what drew my interest was the faint yellow light that appeared in the room afterwards.

I was unsure what was happening inside the room, but I was curious to find out. I walked slowly towards the source of the light.

It turned out to be the main office of the camp. Not exactly an exciting place. The door to the office was open, but the screen door was closed (to keep the insects out). While my initial excitement had all but evaporated, I figured since I had already made the effort to walk over here, I might as well take a look through the screen door.

There was a man using a projector to test slide shows that were to be used during the gospel camps. I am naturally curious about new things, so I stood outside the door to watch the slides. But my attention gradually shifted from the pictures themselves to the man who was projecting them.

This man scratched his back and shuffled around his seat non-stop during the slide shows. I immediately thought that he must have ADHD. It's not a stretch to say that he looked and behaved like a monkey.

This man, who is now my husband, was Barnabas, who incidentally was born in the year of the monkey (in the Chinese Zodiac). I really believe he has ADHD. He rarely stops to rest. Even now when he is at home, he spends the majority of his time sitting in front of his computer reading and working. His friends around the world often ask him how he can reply to their emails so quickly, not only during the day where he is, but also in the dead of night. My two sons did not inherit this side of Barnabas. However, looking at my oldest granddaughter is like looking at a real-life miniature Barnabas.

Perhaps due to Barnabas' home life in his childhood, he did not socialize well with others at the time. His adoptive mother did not allow him much contact with the outside world. With the exception of his time at school, he spent virtually the remainder of his time working at home or at the wet market. Why did his birth parents abandon him? Why did his adoptive mother treat him this way? There was no way for him to understand, and no person for him to inquire as to the reasons why.

For a person who grew up alone in such an oppressive environment, it is of no surprise that he grew up to be a rather solitary person who did not like to talk. However, due to God's grace and protection, a pure heart that truly loved people remained in Barnabas, in spite of the pain and anger that he faced daily. Because of his personal experiences, he is able to empathize with and comfort those who have faced similar trials.

To receive the shaping and molding of God sounds radiant and glorious. However, if it were up to each individual, how many of us would volunteer to be shaped and molded this way?

When I had only known Barnabas for two weeks, one of his supervisors said something about him that left a deep impression on me: "Other than working, Barnabas eats. That's more or less all he does." However, after some observation, I found that Barnabas also enjoyed playing different types of sports. Working and residing at a camp grants its staff access to all of its recreational facilities. He would play basketball with other staff members after every meal. He was actually quite good back then.

As for children, he had shown little interest toward them. Because he was still learning to socialize with others, he often appeared moody or upset, since that was the face that he wore for much of his childhood. Naturally, children avoided him too.

Barnabas had repeatedly stated his lack of affection toward children, and I also thought the responsibility of teaching and disciplining children was a heavy one. I was quite happy, just the two of us, with a lot of time to ourselves.

We planned on being a childless couple, but God did not allow it. After three years of marriage, our first unplanned son was born. Two years later, it happened again with our second son, also unplanned.

The arrival of our two sons really helped Barnabas to understand love. It also helped me understand that most men don't love other people's babies, but absolutely love their own flesh and blood. Because of his great love, our two sons have favored their father more ever since they were young. Even my three-year-old granddaughter is the same way. If Grandpa asks for a bite of her food, she will happily share with him, but she treats me sometimes a bit differently: One time, she was eating ice cream. I wanted her to share some with me. She immediately said "no." I kept on insisting, and she finally and reluctantly said "ok." But I did not expect what happened next: she took a little spoon and gave me an amount of ice cream equal to a grain of rice. I said to her: "why so little?" She then immediately took a big spoonful of ice cream from her own little spoon and put it into her mouth, while slowly handing me the other little spoon with ice cream the size of a grain of rice. How could this be? But I have been well trained for over thirty years, and I have no problem with it. As I know I don't give as much as Barnabas does, perhaps this treatment towards me is only fair!

Barnabas and I are polar opposites in many ways. For example, when people first meet us, most would think that I'm the warm and welcoming one while Barnabas would be difficult to approach. However, after a while, people realize that while Barnabas may appear cold on the outside at first, he is actually rather warm on the inside after you get to know him. Whereas for me, I would much prefer to keep my social circle small and have time by myself most of the time. Home is my favorite place.

Another example: Barnabas is hard-working while I am lazy. There is something I often like to say: "If I could lay down, I would not sit. If I could stand, I would not walk." But Barnabas is willing to put up with me and work a little more. To this day, I cannot understand why he has tolerated me for so long. However, I respect the unique ways that God has made us.

There is a famous saying: "*Men are from Mars, women are from Venus.*" We are different and we must find ways to work together, especially as husband and wife. Barnabas and I have been working at it for decades. Like any loving couple that has lasted this long, our relationship has endured countless tears, as well as times of patience, forgiveness and understanding.

Even after having been married for thirty-nine years, things are still constantly changing. Through the molding of the Lord, Barnabas has become an able preacher. I, in particular, enjoy his sermons in Cantonese. He always seeks to improve and do his best to prepare, and his words have become a blessing to many.

Due to his childhood experiences, he empathizes and shares in others' heartaches. If time allows, he would sincerely and patiently listen to the sharing of anyone he comes across. He obviously cannot offer tangible advice every time, but he would always offer his time, along with words of encouragement and support. People often just need to vent their frustrations and be heard. The time that Barnabas gives to others also becomes a blessing to them.

Because of the love that Barnabas has demonstrated for our

sons, our sons understand that love comes from God and they, in turn, love all those around them. Because of love, they willfully and joyfully serve alongside their father in ministry. Under the example of their father, our sons have matured in their personalities, faith and daily conduct. I pray that they continue to seek after the Lord, and be sources of blessings to others in due time.

—MARGARET

———————————

Throughout our years in ministry, people have often asked my father the following question: "How do you get your sons to serve and work with you?"

It is an impossible question to answer, for it is impossible to anticipate one's motivation and expectation in asking that question, of which there are countless combinations.

However, as one of his sons, I can indeed say this: I work alongside my father and family because God called every single one of us to do so. As a husband, father, and leader of our ministry, Barnabas has always directed us toward our Father—to seek after His will, heed His calling and cultivate a relationship with Him. He submits to the way God shapes His servants for His kingdom, rather than imposing his own methods and timetable toward his own ends. He fixes his sight on heavenly and eternal endeavors, not earthly and temporary pursuits. Perhaps most importantly, he demonstrates his beliefs through words and deeds in every facet of his daily life.

Know who your eternal Father is, and follow Him and Him alone. Maintain steadfast obedience to His eternal call, while abstaining from stealing His rightful glory. Deny yourself, take up your cross, and follow Him. That is my father's greatest legacy and the single greatest gift I have received.

May our Father's unyielding love carry you through your

greatest triumphs and darkest hours, as my father has testified.

—JAMES*

———————

I'd always thought I'd live an idyllic, comfortable suburban life in the US, but a trip to China changed that thought, perhaps forever.

Growing up in the US, I was the type of teenager who drove a minivan, binge watched TV, and played computer games. Everything I had known was the American norm. The thought of what I wanted to do in life had never crossed my mind, other than not wanting to drive that minivan as a freshman in college.

"Are we there yet?" I remembered mumbling to my dad that summer, but we weren't on a road trip to NYC—we were riding in a car to the middle of nowhere in rural China. My father wanted my brother and I to experience the House Church in China. I had no idea what we were in for, but we got out of the car and entered a village home. We walked into a bedroom, the pastor pushed aside the bed, and there was a staircase that led underground. "Cool!" I thought, I had seen something like that on the news: "DEA busts a narcotics smuggling tunnel at the Mexican border." But no, we stepped into an underground seminary, where Christians would spend months at a time literally underground, surrounded by hardened mud, to study God's Word in secrecy. That trip, I met Chinese Christians that exemplified the true meaning of "taking up the cross and surrendering everything to follow Jesus," things that I'd often heard my youth pastor say.

It was during that trip to China that God gave me a calling in life: to serve the House Church in China—those who are willing to suffer and give up everything to proclaim the gospel—all while being an ocean away from American suburbia.

Take a journey with my father through the chapters of this book, and you will see the way God has worked in my father's life is nothing but miracle after miracle, from birth to the present day. You'll meet my father, a humble servant-leader who is willing to do anything for those around him, has taken up the cross, is doing amazing things all across China, and has stories to tell. It is my hope that these stories will change you too, just as they have changed me, perhaps forever.

—NATHAN*

An underground Bible school (We helped to install the lights)

———————

When I first met Barnabas in person, I had already been dating his older son for about a year. I had heard so much about him—about his calling to serve the House Church in China, his decisions to live by faith, and his tireless and humble work in service to God and others. I have been privileged to call him my father-in-law now for the past eleven years.

Barnabas has been a great role model for me of what true faith should look like. If he has an opportunity to do God's work but lacks the funds, he trusts that God will provide the necessary donations. If he sees a need and he can help, he will step in and personally serve others, physically and/or financially. If someone calls him in the middle of the night, he will wake up to listen and pray with them. When others or I have acted sinfully, he has shown grace.

I hope that the stories in this book will encourage and inspire us to be more like Barnabas—to live out our faith in action, to show God's love to others, and to boldly serve God wherever He may be leading us.

—CHRISTINE*

In life and family, Barnabas is a true servant of God, serving wholeheartedly and tirelessly. This collection of stories tells a personal tale that not only further illuminates the depth of Barnabas' commitment and passion for the church in China, but also the genuine desire of the Chinese people to seek after Jesus. This is an open book about Barnabas, allowing the reader to know him as a man at home, and also as a leader in ministry. It is truly an enjoyable read that will also bring the reader more than a few chuckles.

—DIANA*

PHOTOS

The man in the middle is my adoptive father

Aerial photo of a fishing village in Tai Po, 1950s

Fishermen in Tai Po, 1950s

When I was a teenager in Hong Kong

Playing with dogs at a Christian camp in Hong Kong

Photos from house churches inside China

Photos from house churches inside China

Photos from house churches inside China

HC Ministry Training Seminar

Underground Bible schools

ENDNOTES

i   Binyan Liu and Perry Link, *People or Monsters?: And Other Stories and Reportage from China after Mao* (Bloomington: Indiana Univ. Press, 1988).

ii   Binyan Liu and Hong Zhu, *A Higher Kind of Loyalty: a Memoir by China's Foremost Journalist* (New York: Pantheon Books, 1990).

iii   Havel Václav and John Keane, *The Power of the Powerless: Citizens against the State in Eastern Europe* (London: Hutchinson, 1985).

iv   You can easily find information about this study online at the Harvard University website. I read the final report when it was released a few years ago and found it very insightful. https://dataverse.harvard.edu/dataset.xhtml?persistentId=-doi:10.7910/DVN/48WRX9

v   Stossel, Scott (May 2013). "What Makes Us Happy, Revisited: A new look at the famous Harvard study of what makes people thrive." The Atlantic. Archived from the original on 7 June 2017.

vi   Eckholm, Erik. "China Protests Planned Canonization of 120." The New York Times. The New York Times, September 27, 2000. https://www.nytimes.com/2000/09/27/world/china-protests-planned-canonization-of-120.html.

vii   "Three Self Church." THREE SELF CHURCH - Probing China's Three Self Patriotic Church. https://www.billionbibles.com/china/three-self-church.html.

viii   "Christian Persecution In China," CHRISTIAN PERSECUTION IN CHINA - Current Status, accessed May 21, 2020, https://www.billionbibles.com/china/christian-persecution-in-china.html.

ix   Simon and Garfunkel, Paul Simon, and Bud Scoppa. 2001. *Sounds of Silence*.

Leave Nothing Left website:
http://www.leavenothingleft.com

Contact us at: info@leavenothingleft.com

Printed in Great Britain
by Amazon

48229297R00139